SHADOW
STATE

SHADOW STATE

THE POLITICS OF STATE CAPTURE

IVOR CHIPKIN & MARK SWILLING

WITH

HAROON BHORAT | MBONGISENI BUTHELEZI | SIKHULEKILE DUMA
HANNAH FRIEDENSTEIN | LUMKILE MONDI | CAMAREN PETER
NICKY PRINS | MZUKISI QOBO

WITS UNIVERSITY PRESS

Published in South Africa by:
Wits University Press
1 Jan Smuts Avenue
Johannesburg 2001

www.witspress.co.za

First published 2018

http://dx.doi.org.10.18772/22018072125

978-1-77614-212-5 (Print)
978-1-77614-213-2 (Web PDF)
978-1-77614-214-9 (EPUB)

Copy editor: Pat Tucker
Proofreader: Lee Smith
Indexer: Mirie van Rooyen
Cover design: Fire and Lion
Typesetter: Newgen
Typeset in 9.5 point ScalaPro

Contents

List of figures and tables

Acronyms and abbreviations

ACSA Airports Company South Africa
ANC African National Congress
ANCYL African National Congress Youth League
ASGISA Accelerated and Shared Growth Initiative for South Africa
B-BBEE broad-based black economic empowerment
BBC Black Business Council
BEE black economic empowerment
BLSA Business Leadership South Africa
CEO chief executive officer
Cosatu Congress of South African Trade Unions
CSIR Council for Scientific and Industrial Research
DTI Department of Trade and Industry
Gear Growth, Employment and Redistribution
IDC Industrial Development Corporation
NDP National Development Plan
NEC National Executive Committee
NGO non-governmental organisation
NMOS National Macro Organisation of State
NNEECC National Nuclear Energy Executive Coordination Committee
NPA National Prosecuting Authority
PARI Public Affairs Research Institute
Prasa Passenger Rail Agency of South Africa
RDP Reconstruction and Development Programme
SAA South African Airways
SABC South African Broadcasting Corporation
SACC South African Council of Churches

SACP South African Communist Party
SAPO South African Post Office
SARS South African Revenue Service
SASSA South African Social Security Agency
SITA State Information Technology Agency
SOE state-owned enterprise

Key terms

Corruption and state capture

Corruption tends to be an individual action that occurs in exceptional cases, facilitated by a loose network of corrupt players. It is informally organised, fragmented and opportunistic. State capture is systemic and well organised by people who have an established relationship with one another. It involves repeated transactions, often on an increasing scale.

Our focus in this book is not on small-scale looting but on accessing and redirecting rents (defined below) away from their intended targets into private hands. In order to succeed, the perpetrators need high-level political protection, including from law enforcement agencies; intense loyalty to one another; a climate of fear; and the elimination of competitors.

The aim of state capture is not to bypass rules to get away with corrupt behaviour; the term 'corruption' obscures the politics that frequently informs these processes, treating it as a moral or cultural pathology. Yet corruption, as is often the case in South Africa, is frequently the result of a political conviction that the formal 'rules of the game' are rigged against specific constituencies and it is therefore legitimate to break them. The aim of state capture is to change the formal and informal rules of the game, legitimise them and select the players who are allowed to participate.

Power elite

We use the notion of a 'power elite' to refer to a relatively well-structured network of people located in government, state institutions, state-owned enterprises (SOEs), private businesses, security agencies, traditional leaders, family networks and the governing party. The defining feature of membership of this group is direct (and even indirect) access (either consistently or intermittently) to the inner sanctum of power to influence decisions. It is not a ruling class as such, although it can see itself as acting in the interests of an existing class or, as in the South African case, a new black business class in the making. Nor is it just the political–bureaucratic leadership of the state, which is too fragmented to mount a political project reliably.

The power elite, which is not necessarily directed by a strong strategic centre, includes groups that are to some extent competing for access to the inner sanctum and the opportunity to control rents. It exercises its influence through both formal and informal means. However, what unites the power elite is the desire to manage effectively the symbiotic relationship between the constitutional and shadow states. In order to do this, and in broad terms, it organises itself loosely around a 'patron' or 'strongman', who has direct access to resources and under whom a layer of 'elites' forms. These elites dispense the patronage, which is then managed by another layer of 'brokers' or 'middlemen'.

Repurposing

The repurposing of state institutions is the organised process of reconfiguring the way in which a given institution is structured, governed, managed and funded so that it serves a different purpose from its formal mandate. Understanding state capture purely as a vehicle for looting does not explain the full extent of the political project that enables it. Institutions are captured for a purpose beyond looting, namely consolidating political power to ensure longer-term survival, the maintenance of a political coalition and its validation by an ideology that masks private enrichment with references to public benefit.

Rents and rent seeking

Development is a process that is consciously instigated when states adopt policies to reallocate resources, directly and/or indirectly, to redress the wrongs of the past and to create modern, transformed, industrialised economies that can support the wellbeing of society. To achieve this, state institutions must be used to reallocate resources from one group to another, or to support one group to enable it to overcome the disadvantages of the past. These allocations can be called *beneficial rents*.

However, once the state takes measures that result in a flow of potentially beneficial rents to specific economic actors (whether these are businesses, households or public institutions), there is competition to access these flows and this creates the conditions for rent seeking.

While legal, ethical rent seeking, such as lobbying or legal interventions, bene-fits certain groups, rent seeking can also be corrupt and lead ultimately to state cap-ture and repurposing. Corrupt rent-seeking behaviour can undermine the state's development agenda by diverting resources into the hands of unproductive elites. It follows that if beneficial rents are necessary for development to take place, a system is needed to counteract the inevitable competition to access them from being cor-rupted by those who gain leverage via political access, bribery, promises of future returns, and so on.

The literature on neopatrimonialism provides examples of countries that managed to accelerate development by effectively deploying beneficial rents to boost specific economic actors.[1] Limiting corruption was a key element of these programmes. The most successful ones tended to be guided by a long-term devel-opmental vision and to centralise control of rents so as to limit overly compet-itive and destructive rent seeking. They never eliminated corruption, but they prevented it from corroding the development process. Centralised rent manage-ment can, of course, also be corrupted by power elites who use it to eliminate lower-level competitors in order to further enrich themselves and entrench their power positions.

Symbiotic relationship between the constitutional state and the shadow state

Drawing on the well-developed literature on neopatrimonialism, we refer to the emergence of a symbiotic relationship between the constitutional state and the shadow state.[2] The constitutional state is the formalised constitutional, legislative and jurisprudential framework of rules that governs what government and state institutions can and cannot do. The shadow state is the networks of relationships that cross-cut and bind a specific group of people who need to act together in secre-tive ways so that they can either effectively hide, actively deny or consciously 'not know' that which contradicts their formal roles in the constitutional state. This is a world where deniability is valued, culpability is distributed and trust is maintained through mutually binding fear.

Unsurprisingly, therefore, the shadow state is not only the space for extra-legal action facilitated by criminal networks, but also a place where key security and intel-ligence actions are coordinated. As extra-legal activity becomes more important, ensuring a compliant security and intelligence apparatus becomes a key priority.

What matters is the symbiosis between the two, which is what the rent-seeking power elite emerges to achieve.

The symbiosis that binds the power elite consists of the transactions between those located within the constitutional state and those located outside the constitutional state who have been granted preferential access via these networks to the decision-making processes within the constitutional state. These networks have their own rules and logic that endow key players within them with the authority to influence decisions, allocate resources and appoint key personnel. In the South African context the Gupta and Zuma families (popularly referred to as the 'Zuptas') have comprised the most powerful node, which has enabled them to determine how the networks operate and who has access. They depend on a range of secondary nodes clustered around key individuals in state departments, SOEs and regulatory agencies.

Radical economic transformation

Although the official African National Congress (ANC) ideology of radical economic transformation is ill defined and lacks a discernible conceptual framework, such transformation is needed if the promise of 1994 is to be realised. Too little has been done to this end. However, because the notion of radical economic transformation is apparently used to mask a political project that enriches the few, subverts South Africa's democratic and constitutional system, weakens state institutions and expatriates capital overseas, we differentiate between the ideological goal and the real intentions of ANC policy documents. We argue that a new economic consensus will be required that will entail very radical change, but without subverting the constitutional state. For radical economic transformation to become the basis of a new economic consensus it must, in practice, be achieved within the existing constitutional order and an appropriately enacted legislative framework. Contrary to what is stated in ANC policy documents, the power elite professes a commitment to radical economic transformation but sees the constitutional order and legislative framework as obstacles to transformation.

Political project

The political project of the Zuma-centred power elite is the manner in which power is intentionally deployed in ways that serve the interests of this elite. This project is legitimised, in turn, by an ideology that is repeatedly articulated by a specific (but ever-shifting) political coalition of interests (one that includes both the power elite and wider networks). Jacob Zuma's abuse of power has enabled strategies that are aimed at promoting corrupt rent-seeking practices by preferred networks and the consolidation of power by an inner core around Zuma.

Clientelism

Clientelism is the exchange of goods and services for political support, often involving an implicit or explicit quid pro quo. It involves an asymmetric relationship – that is, a relationship of unequal power – among groups of political actors described as patrons, brokers and clients.

Notes and references

1   For a useful overview see Kelsall, T. 2013. *Business, Politics and the State in Africa*. London: Zed Press.
2   Kelsall. 2013. *Business, Politics*.

Acknowledgements

We would like to acknowledge the support of a wide range of individuals and institutions without whom this publication would not have been possible. However, the arguments, opinions and conclusions presented in the text belong solely to the authors.

We first acknowledge the contributions of those who took risks to talk to us and provide information. We also want to acknowledge the universities and their respective administrations that enabled the researchers to collaborate with each other to do this work, specifically the Universities of Cape Town, Stellenbosch, the Witwatersrand and Johannesburg. We want to acknowledge three institutions that collaborated to manage the funds and provide logistical and office support for the researchers: the Centre for Complex Systems in Transition at the University of Stellenbosch, the Public Affairs Research Institute at the University of the Witwatersrand and the Sustainability Institute. Finally, we want to acknowledge the Open Society Foundation for providing the funding required to conduct the research and publish the original report on which this book is based. They had faith in our capabilities to build a team and publish a report of our findings in a very short space of time.

Foreword

Mcebisi Jonas

In March 2017, a few weeks before Pravin Gordhan and I were removed from the Ministry of Finance by former President Jacob Zuma, I met with Professor Mark Swilling at the Sustainability Institute in Stellenbosch. Mark and I had known each other and worked together for many years and he is someone I had come to rely on in the academic community. I had asked Mark to meet with me to discuss my increasing concern about the polarised, and frankly deliberately rudimentary, debate that was emerging on state capture. As the pressure was mounting on the perpetrators of state capture, so they were ratcheting up the narrative that this was a political project to displace white monopoly capital – a project of radical economic transformation to free black economic empowerment from the insidious forces of what was increasingly referred to as white monopoly capital. I was also concerned that as South Africans scrambled to grasp the meaning of state capture, there was a propensity to simplify it to 'corruption'.

It was clear that if we as a nation failed to understand the significance of what we were facing, we would also have to accept that our hard-won democracy would become something that we talked about as lost in our lifetime. That was the danger that we faced.

My concern, like that of many South Africans, was multi-layered – I was distressed at a personal and professional level, and in my case, also as a member of the ruling African National Congress (ANC). When the ANC came to power in 1994, we promised that we would ensure that progressively we would destroy the apartheid-era bureaucracy, and that we would build a capable state to drive forward the agenda of liberating our people and deepening development in our country. It was becoming apparent to me that the significant progress we had made since 1994 in transforming our state institutions into vehicles for service delivery and development, and building the constitutional foundations of our democracy, was under severe threat from the gluttonous tentacles of a small but powerful business and political elite.

By the time Mark and I met, there was already significant pushback against state capture from various sites of accountability, including but not limited to investigative journalists and the media in general, civil society and the judiciary. But we were still observing each new example of state capture as a separate event, denying the connection between them. We were failing to join the dots. And what was missing was the voice of the academic community – the dot joiners.

What was also apparent at that point in time was that state capture was not corruption – it was exponentially more complex, and indeed we were at risk of over-looking a fundamental threat to our egalitarian project if we thought we were only dealing with corruption. This is not to deny the seriousness of corruption, which also undermines development; but through state capture, the rule-making process itself was being captured, legitimising the theft of our nation. This goes to the fundamental difference between corruption and state capture – for the latter, many of its activities may be legal, hiding the gradual, well-organised, but often terminal nature of its ultimate impact.

It was clear that we needed a dispassionate understanding of what was unfolding before us. We needed a factual and analytical narrative. And so I met Mark, as an old friend, to ask him to convene a meeting of academic minds. He did this, colloquially calling the group the State Capacity Research Project; this group moved into and occupied this space, almost without a break for eight weeks (unheard of for academics!), and re-emerged with the report titled *Betrayal of the Promise*, now published in edited form as this book. The gravity of what they discovered and distilled into this comprehensible, but disquieting, read is best encapsulated in what they termed the 'silent coup' – the betrayal of the 1994 promise.

The publication of the report on 18 May 2017 was unintentionally well-timed. Two weeks before, the South African Council of Churches (SACC) – which had become a spearhead of the anti-state capture fightback – had released the draft findings of their 'Unburdening Panel', a process they had established to create a safe and trusted space for perpetrators and victims of state capture to come forward. The academics had worked closely with the SACC, having discovered a consistency between the patterns of their findings. The Unburdening Panel draft report was the first portal for the public to begin understanding the gravity of the state capture crisis, the *Betrayal of the Promise* report followed, and a few days later, the first #GuptaLeaks were broken by the media.

And so, in many ways, this publication – book-ended by the Unburdening Panel report and the #GuptaLeaks – marked a turning point in the popular front against state capture. The dots were being joined.

The importance of the present book lies in its power of reshaping the state capture narrative. For the first time, South Africans have been able to grasp the horrifying reality of what we were facing. But the book must also stand as a strong warning against complacency. We are no longer standing on the brink, but as William Faulkner once wrote, 'The past isn't dead and buried. In fact, it isn't even past.' We do not need to remind ourselves here of the deep racial, economic and social wounds that mar our country on a daily basis, but we do need to remind ourselves that state capture was simply a symptom of these deep wounds, and they can no longer be plastered over.

Prologue

In mid-March 2017 Mark Swilling was travelling in business class to Johannesburg from Cape Town. He was in an aisle seat and Mcebisi Jonas, then the deputy minister of finance, was in the aisle seat on the opposite side. They had last worked together in the early 1990s when Jonas was active in the Eastern Cape, coordinating a forum focused on appropriate economic development strategies for that province.

After exchanging the usual 'comradely' greetings, Jonas gave Mark his iPad and said, 'Read this and tell me what you think.' He had already by then refused a R600 million bribe offered to him by the Gupta brothers, a move, knowing him, that came as no surprise to Mark. Mark then read a paper that in subsequent months would be read again and again by the research team – the first comprehensive overview of what all South Africans would soon come to call 'state capture'. This was the paper that Mark gave to Ivor Chipkin at their first meeting to discuss the assembly of a team that would eventually produce the *Betrayal of the Promise* report. Needless to say, it was a paper that needed to be kept totally confidential.

Those who read this paper in those dark days of 2017 were all profoundly disturbed by it, and particularly frightened by the fact that it was written by a member of the Cabinet. Jonas candidly shared with Mark his deep pessimism about what was going on. He took down Mark's phone number, promising to call him. A few days later Mark got a call from Jonas asking to meet at the Sustainability Institute at Stellenbosch University.

Jonas arrived and the first thing Mark noticed was that he gave his phone to the driver before entering the building. The two hours that followed were among the most remarkable and surprising Mark had experienced since 1994. Jonas spoke about what he thought was going on. Mark desperately wanted to tape what he was saying, or take notes, but he had no idea why Jonas was there and what he needed done. Mark just absorbed what he could, describing the experience to Ivor a few days later as the sum of all fears.

When Jonas finished briefing him, Mark asked why he had come to see him. Jonas wanted to know what the academics were doing about the situation. He said, 'Our concern is that the narrative is about corruption – that creates the wrong impression. South Africa needs to understand that this is a systemic problem – it is a political project to capture the state. The narrative needs to change.' He wanted to make it clear that this was not just a criminal enterprise. It was a political project.

Mark then suggested setting up a group of academics who could pull together all the information and publish a report that, to use Pravin Gordhan's now famous phrase uttered at a press conference when he and Jonas were eventually fired two weeks later, 'joined the dots'. Jonas's immediate reaction seemed negative: 'We don't have the funds for that.' After Mark said the academics would raise the funds, Jonas agreed. Subsequently they would meet almost weekly, and a network of people within and outside the state was built up who provided the key information that was used in the report and in this book.

Mark's first move after this initial meeting with Jonas was to contact Ivor, talking via the Signal app, and Ivor's immediate response was 'I'm in'. But he had independently established links with former National Treasury and South African Revenue Service (SARS) officials, and he warned Mark that this was dangerous work. What followed was a flurry of meetings with a number of prominent academics to invite them to join the group. Several of the academics contacted refused to participate, which reflected the atmosphere of the time. Those were dark days, when fear was used to fragment oppositional thinking and the Zuma-led power elite projected an image of supreme confidence, legitimised by the unwavering loyalty of the governing party, and by populist rhetoric like 'white monopoly capital' and 'radical economic transformation', language that was broadcast widely by the Gupta-financed campaign orchestrated by Bell Pottinger Private, a UK-based multinational public relations company.

However, a core group of people who had never worked together gelled to co-write the report that was published two months later as *Betrayal of the Promise: How South Africa Is Being Stolen*, calling itself the State Capacity Research Project. Mark and Ivor, as well as the other members of the research team, were all familiar with the complex political dynamics of the real world of everyday governance. Mark had cut his teeth doing solid political analysis as a young academic in the 1980s, analysing the apartheid state's 'counter-insurgency' strategy during the first State of Emergency and its 'winning-hearts-and-minds' strategy during the second State of Emergency. Both Ivor and Mark had subsequently analysed the dynamics of transition to democracy and the complex process of building a developmental, capable state administration. Sikhulekile Duma, a participant in Mark's master's degree programme, had experience as a #FeesMustFall student leader, which brought in a perspective from the younger generation. All the other authors had hands-on experience of public sector governance, including economists Lumkile Mondi, who had worked at a senior level in SOEs, and Mzukisi Qobo, who had been a government official.

While all the members of the research team had a general knowledge of the institutional meltdown taking place since Jacob Zuma had become president of South Africa, when Jonas spoke all were deeply shocked by the sheer audacity of the Zuma–Gupta networks and how they operated.

We had to assemble a communications system reminiscent of the struggle years, when research aimed at supporting the mass democratic movement had to be protected from the security police. The strategy was not to try hide everything, because if you did, the gap between intense activity and absence of a work programme inevitably attracted attention. This meant hiding the ten per cent of our work that was really sensitive. Using Google Docs and apps like Signal to communicate, rather than WhatsApp, became key. During the 1980s, when the task was exposing counter-insurgency and the 'winning-hearts-and-minds' strategy, the greatest challenge was setting up secret meetings with sources in the system. These had to be face-to-face and fairly regular. Today it is not necessary to meet a source. Messaging sources via Signal and collaboration with them via Google Docs, using false email addresses, works extremely well. Cellphones were switched off and removed from the locations where meetings were taking place. Documents were exchanged via a Google account that everyone had access to, and where files were saved in unsent emails.

There was a constant sense of danger. The Public Affairs Research Institute (PARI) offices were broken into, and nothing stolen. Someone shot a bullet through Ivor's car window. Some members of the research team noticed surveillance vehicles outside their residences, and some started to worry about the safety of their children. Ominous statements by then Minister of State Security David Mahlobo about foreign funding, non-governmental organisations (NGOs) and regime change reinforced the sense of déjà vu, and a statement heard often was 'it's like the struggle years all over again'.

Significantly, the academics who did get involved were relieved when their respective senior managers were extremely supportive. Fortunately the University of the Witwatersrand (Wits), the University of Johannesburg, the University of Cape Town (UCT) and the University of Stellenbosch were established universities that had not been browbeaten into political loyalty. We sympathised with those who felt less protected and had therefore turned down the invitation to be part of the group.

After the Cabinet reshuffle in late March 2017 resulted in the firing of Gordhan and Jonas, we had to quickly reposition our work. Until this point, our strategy had been focused on the building up of a narrative that effectively defended the National Treasury against capture by strengthening the hand of a group of ministers who were starting to coordinate a campaign against the Zuma-led power elite. After the reshuffle, the strategy shifted to a focus on compiling a report for broad public consumption that would reinforce the convening of some sort of multi-stakeholder national dialogue, possibly leading to the formation of a popular front.

This eventually led to our collaboration with the South African Council of Churches (SACC), including a fascinating session with Archbishop Thabo Makgoba at his residence in Constantia, attended by many leading clerics. Powerful echoes of the struggle years overwhelmed us, especially when we looked across the table at the Reverend Frank Chikane, with whom Mark had last worked during the Soweto rent boycott in the early 1990s.

Remarkably, the group of academics who co-wrote the report quickly found common ground and made space in their schedules for getting the work done. The most significant moment in the process was the week we all spent together at the Centre for Complex Systems in Transition in Stellenbosch. While the research team worked on the components of the story, key people, including Jonas, came in for a day or two to make their contributions. By the end of the week the storyline had emerged, together with a work programme that defined who would write which chapter. Without this period of intense engagement and long hours of discussion it would not have been possible to reach the clarity needed to bring out a credible report by May 2017.

After discussions with the SACC it was agreed that the report would be launched at a national consultative event organised by the Council. This was supposed to be a multi-stakeholder event. However, for two reasons that did not happen. Firstly, our lawyer advised against it, saying a lot of work was still needed to change the phrasing of the report if we wanted to avoid a serious defamation case. I learnt a key lesson: asserting something about someone supported by references as if it is true is defamation, whereas the way to avoid defamation is to say 'if this report is true, then ...'. This slight twist in the wording means you are admitting you did not do the original research, and you are not confirming what has been reported. All we had to do was draw conclusions from a reported fact that had not been publicly countered by a credible source, nor checked by us. Thus it would be the original report, not our own text, that carried the burden of proof. This saved our bacon.

The second reason, as we explain in the Introduction to this book, was that the envisaged SACC event had turned into a launch of a different 'report', one whose purpose was to reveal the results of a separate 'unburdening' process that the SACC had initiated for church members compromised by the process of state capture.

At an event convened by the team at PARI, we launched our report a week later in the auditorium of the Wits School of Governance. It was covered on prime-time TV and extensively reported in the national press. All the co-authors were involved in radio and TV talk shows, and delivered keynote addresses at several important events. The most notable of these was the National Conference of the South African Communist Party (SACP), addressed by Ivor and Sikhulekile. Several Cabinet ministers were present, as was Jesse Duarte, the deputy secretary general of the ANC at the time.

Two days after the launch the #GuptaLeaks material – an enormous quantity of anonymously released emails relating to interactions and transactions between individuals involved with the Gupta family – broke into the public domain. We were offered access to this material prior to it being made public, but after convening urgently at a meeting at Cape Town International Airport, we decided this was not our role as academics and refused the offer. We felt it was too dangerous for us to make use of the emails, and that in any case this was a job better done by journalists. Fortunately the #GuptaLeaks emails, when they did hit the public domain, confirmed our argument and analysis. These two events, together with the SACC's presentation a week earlier, triggered a groundswell that effectively changed the public narrative from one of isolated instances of corruption into one about a systemic process of state capture coordinated by a power elite committed to an explicit political project. We called this the silent coup.

The key lesson this process holds for us is about the role we academics must play in society and in public discourse. We go about our business assembling research projects and publishing in professional journals. Some of us are engaged at project level doing really good work. But more of us need to use our status and skills to speak truth to power. Society tends to have faith in us. However, funding requirements these days force many academics to conduct inter- or transdisciplinary research with societal stakeholders and policy makers. Quite often these collaborative projects prevent academics from 'speaking out' against poor governance, because this would put at risk the relationships that are needed to make the project work. 'Speaking truth to power' becomes a casualty when 'policy relevance' becomes sacrosanct. In more consensual societies this might not be a problem but it would be counterproductive in a society like ours, where deep divisions and sustained conflict are the norm.

This book, like the original report, is inspired by the classic belief in the role of the organic intellectual who must speak truth to power, no matter the price. However, unlike in the past, the complexity of today's world requires academics to collaborate and to build the mutual trust that makes collaboration work effectively. Without collaboration, the vast quantities of information that stem from a wide variety of sources cannot be effectively assembled. Teams need to be formed comprising people with a range of different (but possibly overlapping) networks that make it possible not only to access diverse flows of information, but also to verify key pieces of information from different perspectives and sources. The metaphor for this type of collaborative work would be a kind of ideational meshwork that makes it possible to capture and interpret a much larger flow of information and ideas than would otherwise be possible for the lone researcher using traditional data-trawling methods.

Making collaboration work, however, is no easy task. It means creating a space defined by a strong shared vision, but with soft boundaries that allow the space to morph over time in accordance with the preferences and inclinations of the team. The identity this generates allows members to feel they can take initiative without hierarchical decision-making, and that others can easily join. For example, after reading the report in a single sitting, Professor Anton Eberhard of the University of Cape Town made contact with us to ask if he could do a case study of Eskom and publish it in the name of the State Capacity Research Project. There were other similar approaches. However, this kind of amoebic form only really works when there is mutual trust and respect. This is not always the case, which is why a capacity to facilitate conflict resolution is also a requirement for this way of working.

Mark Swilling and Ivor Chipkin

Introduction

The new struggle for democracy: how civil society fought back against state capture

In the classical texts, tyranny, as opposed to despotism, refers to a form of government that breaks its own rules. This is a useful starting point for discussing political developments in South Africa in the past ten years and the civil society response to it. The ANC government under Jacob Zuma became more and more tyrannical as it set itself up against the Constitution and the rule of law in an effort to capture the state.

In moves reminiscent of events in the 1980s, independent journalists, social movements, trade unions, legal aid centres, NGOs, the churches and some academics have helped mobilise South African society against state capture. A new and varied movement has arisen, bringing together awkward partnerships between ideologically disparate groups and people. What they have nonetheless shared is a broad support for the Constitution, for democracy and for a modern, professional administration, and they are all, broadly speaking, social democratic in orientation.

The publication of the *Betrayal of the Promise* report, on which this book is based, constituted a key moment, helping to provide this movement with a narrative and concepts for expressing a systemic perspective on state capture that helped its readers to, in the words of former Minister of Finance Pravin Gordhan, 'join the dots'.[1]

The particular instance of so-called 'state capture' that we discuss in this book is part of a familiar and recurring pattern in the history of state formation in South Africa. It is, in fact, impossible to understand the evolution of South African politics and statecraft without understanding the deeper dynamics of what we refer to today as state capture. There is a clear and direct line of sight from the origins of the state in the Cape Colony, when it was 'captured' by the Dutch East India Company, through to the era of Cecil Rhodes and 'Milner's Kindergarten' – the name popularly given to the young British civil servants who served under High Commissioner Alfred, Lord Milner – in post-Boer War South Africa.

The world that the first generations of mining magnates, the so-called Randlords, built on the Witwatersrand provided the foundation for the election victory of the National Party in 1948. The post-1948 state actively supported the build-up of Afrikaner capital in a process which effectively captured the state for decades, with the Electricity Supply Commission (Escom, now renamed Eskom) and the South African Railways (now renamed Transnet) at the very centre of that political project.

The corporate capture of the apartheid war- and sanctions-busting machine has been well documented, with arms manufacturer Armscor (renamed Denel after 1994) at its centre. Also well documented is the powerful role played by corporate South Africa during the transition, to ensure that a democratic state could do little to change the basic structure of the economy. This was a form of capture in that powerful elite interests subverted the broad vision of transformation that inspired the mass democratic movement that had brought down the apartheid state.

The most recent instance of state capture has galvanised a broad-based coalition of forces that share a commitment to building an *uncaptured South African state*. This is what our Constitution envisages. The choice must not be between different forms of capture, it must be between capture and no capture. In taking this stand we are going up against the defeatist view on both the left and right that 'the state is always captured, so why the fuss?'

By focusing on this latest instance of state capture we hope to reinforce the movement for a democratic, uncaptured state, thereby ensuring that South Africans will in future regard *all forms of state capture* as totally unacceptable. Indeed, in our view, this is a precondition for inclusive development, despite the fact that there are very few examples of large-scale redistribution of wealth taking place within a democratic framework.

Turning against the Constitution

From about 2010 the South African government started to introduce measures to control the diffusion of information and tacitly regulate the press. In 2011, in the face of impressive opposition, a majority of members of Parliament representing the ruling ANC voted to pass the Protection of State Information Bill, which was especially controversial for giving government officials the right to classify as 'top secret' any government information deemed to be in the 'national interest'.

As activists from the Right2Know Campaign argued over and over again, the definition of the 'national interest' in the Bill was so broad as to exclude virtually nothing from censorship.[2] The Bill also criminalised 'whistleblowing' and investigative journalism by imposing heavy jail sentences on anybody holding 'classified' information. This resonated with the findings of a 2008 Ministerial Review Commission on Intelligence which had found that the mandate of the South African intelligence services was so broadly defined that ordinary democratic activity could be construed as a national security threat.[3]

Eventually, President Jacob Zuma refused to assent to the legislation, halting its passage into law, on the basis that it would fail at the Constitutional Court. It was, nonetheless, symptomatic of a wider trend.

During this period there were concerted efforts to create alternative media platforms more sympathetic to the ANC government. In this regard, a daily newspaper, *The New Age*, was launched in 2010. Owned by the controversial Gupta family (whose activities are discussed in detail in Chapter 4), it has an explicit mandate to present a positive image of the ANC. Today it claims that it provides positive news that is critically constructive. In 2013 the Guptas launched a 24-hour news channel, ANN7, with the same purpose. More recently, as the Zuma administration came under increasing pressure (see below), ANN7 became a more brazenly propaganda channel.

The South African Broadcasting Corporation (SABC), the country's public broadcaster, has an impressive reach. Public radio is the primary source of news and information for the vast majority of South Africans. In 2011 Hlaudi Motsoeneng, who had been employed at the SABC since 1995, was appointed acting SABC chief operating officer. In 2014 the public protector, an institution established in terms of Chapter 9 of South Africa's Constitution to protect the rights of citizens against abuses by government, found that Motsoeneng had been illegally appointed. He had never finished school and was thus ineligible in terms of the criteria for the post. This notwithstanding, then Communications Minister Faith Muthambi approved his appointment in July 2014. Even after several courts confirmed the finding of the public protector, the executive of the SABC stood by Motsoeneng and when his appointment was finally set aside by the Supreme Court of Appeal, in September 2016, Muthambi intervened to secure him a senior, acting post.

It was not difficult to understand why. Under Motsoeneng the SABC had moved, effectively, to prohibit the reporting of news that was critical of government or was potentially embarrassing. The shift towards a more politicised newsroom at the SABC had started during the Thabo Mbeki administration when the then head of news, Snuki Zikalala, had blacklisted several political commentators who were critical of the government. What happened under Motsoeneng, however, looked more like 'institutional capture'. The policy of the organisation was illegally changed to remove editorial discretion from senior journalists and to grant it instead to the chief operating officer, that is, to Motsoeneng himself. Critical or independent journalists were purged from the organisation.

These events took place in the context of an audacious political project unfolding in other parts of the state as well.

In December 2007, in Polokwane, a provincial town about three hours' drive north of Johannesburg, accumulating tensions within the ruling ANC burst into the open. During the 52nd National Conference of the party Thabo Mbeki failed in his bid to secure a third term as the organisation's president. Jacob Zuma was elected in his stead, coming to power on a wave of resentment of and grievances against the previous administration – not least for allegedly conspiring to destroy Zuma's political career. In September 2008 the ANC 'recalled' Mbeki from his position as South Africa's president. The national election that followed in 2009 saw Jacob Zuma become president of the country as well as of the ANC.

The Polokwane revolt in the ANC was informed by a conviction that economic transformation as pursued during the Mandela and Mbeki eras had produced an anomaly, if not a perversion: a small black elite beholden to white corporate elites, a vulnerable and over-indebted black middle class and a large African majority condemned to unemployment and dependent on welfare handouts to survive. The economic policies of the Mbeki period were widely slated as a self-imposed programme of structural adjustment inspired by neoliberal economic policies. In the wake of Polokwane, and especially after the 2009 election, a search began in earnest for a more 'radical' model of economic transformation. At the time, the Zuma presidency was applauded in 'leftwing' circles for promising a break with the 'neoliberal' policies of the Mbeki years.

The idea of using government's procurement budget to realise social and economic outcomes is not new. It was the backbone of South Africa's 'developmental state' in the 1930s and formed a key platform of the apartheid project, especially in relation to cultivating a class of Afrikaner (nationalist) capitalists.

From about 2011 sections of the ANC and ministers and officials in the Department of Trade and Industry (DTI), supported by elements of organised black business, began referring to 'radical economic transformation'. This was the name given to an ambitious project to leverage the procurement budgets of SOEs to displace established white firms and create new, black-owned and -controlled industrial enterprises.

The two largest SOEs were Eskom (which generated and transmitted electricity across the country) and Transnet (which was responsible for the national bulk rail network). Here was a vision of economic transformation that was not contingent on the reform of 'white businesses' and did not depend on the goodwill of whites to invest in the economy, to employ black people and to treat them as equals. It is easy to see why this vision was profoundly compelling across a range of networks within and outside the ruling party.

From around 2011, however, the project of radical economic transformation increasingly began to set itself up against key state institutions and the constitutional framework. At stake was a critical reading of South Africa's political economy and of the constraints that the transition imposed on economic transformation. This was an analysis emerging from within parts of government and the fringes of the ANC. It resonated closely with the neo-Fanonian readings of South Africa's post-colonial situation that were widely discussed on university campuses, in the Black First Land First grouping and in 'ultra-left' critiques of South Africa's 'elite transition'.[3] It was not the position of the ANC itself. The centrepiece of this critique was the National Treasury – the department of state responsible for government finances, including approval of departmental budgets and allocating monies from the fiscus.

There was one major reason why the National Treasury was a red flag to the project of radical economic transformation: its constitutional mandate placed it on the very sharp horns of a dilemma. In South Africa the terms of public pro-curement are not defined simply in statutes (subject to legislative revision) but are inscribed in the ground law of the country. South Africa's constitutional drafters were prescient, perhaps, about the significance that procurement would assume in the political life of the country after apartheid. The National Treasury, itself a creature of the Constitution, had to try to reconcile black economic empowerment (BEE) with considerations of fair value for the fiscus and for citizens.

When the National Treasury was seen to stall moves to extend the logic of BEE to the SOEs, it came under fierce attack. Indeed, the more the Treasury insisted that government entities proceed in a way that was 'fair, equitable, transparent, competitive and cost-effective', as set down in the Constitution, the more controversial it became.[5] Furthermore, the Treasury was in favour of a conservative fiscal policy, which meant restraining public expenditure relative to gross domestic product rather than running up the deficit. Critics argued that this constrained the state's ability to address the triple challenge of poverty, unemployment and inequality.

As the Zuma administration radicalised and tended towards illegality and straightforward criminality, so it became dependent on managing increasingly complex relations, many of them involving people engaged in unlawful activities. At this time the Zuma administration made moves to establish control over key state institutions, especially those involved in criminal investigations and prosecution: SARS, the Directorate for Priority Crime Investigation (known as the 'Hawks') and the National Prosecuting Authority (NPA). In all these proceedings there was the shadow of South Africa's intelligence services, including the involvement of apartheid-era intelligence officers.

To construct what we call the 'shadow state', two imperatives came into play. Firstly, as the Zuma-centred political project tended towards illegality it was driven into the shadows, with the concomitant risk of the loss of political control. Hence, some form of management system was needed to keep it on course. Secondly, it became necessary to shut down certain investigations and immunise or protect key people from prosecution.

Taken together, the events occurring at SARS and those involving the Hawks (as well as the NPA) suggest that as the Zuma administration became radicalised, and resorted increasingly to unlawful means to pursue its agenda of radical economic transformation, so it was driven to 'capture' and weaken key state institutions. In this way, the political project of the Zuma administration has come at a very heavy price for the capability, integrity and stability of the South African state. This book describes and analyses the primary dynamics of this process.

Civil society reinvigorated

For a long time there was very little organised opposition to these events, but the South African media had largely managed to fend off moves to introduce formal censorship and there was still a legacy of brave, independent investigative journalism.

Largely through the efforts of several such journalists, many of them associated with the amaBhungane Centre for Investigative Journalism, stories broke regularly about the corruption of government officials.

The public protector's *State of Capture* report did a great deal to create public outrage, but the political response was strangely muted.[6] Within the ANC some individuals raised concerns, but, as an organisation, the ANC reliably rallied behind its president. This began to change when then Minister of Finance Nhlanhla Nene was unexpectedly dismissed in December 2015. Financial markets reacted strongly and the South African currency, the rand, plummeted in value.

These events triggered a political response as thousands marched in the streets to protest 'state capture'. Yet the phenomenon remained largely a middle-class one. It was not very difficult for those around the Zuma administration to present such opposition as either the work of political forces opposed to radical change or as working in the service of a foreign agenda.

This began to change after the dismissal in 2017 of the new finance minister, Pravin Gordhan, and his deputy, Mcebisi Jonas – both of whom are highly respected technocrats but also savvy politicians. Opposition to the Zuma administration grew, including from within the ANC.

The problem with the resistance until then, however, was that its analysis of what was going on was superficial. It ultimately fell back on the assumption that the president and his allies were corrupt and motivated by self-interest, or that they were kingpins of a vast network of patronage. Apart from the obvious flaws of such an analysis – it resonated with all sorts of racist clichés about African leaders – it obscured the political project that was at work.

In May 2017 we and several colleagues published a report called *Betrayal of the Promise: How South Africa Is Being Stolen.* We had worked quietly and quickly to gather as much information as possible that was in the public domain in order to 'join the dots', so to speak. The highlights of the argument we made in that report have been referred to above. The centrepiece of the analysis was the way in which the Zuma–Gupta political project turned against the Constitution, the law and South Africa's democratic processes and institutions.

Essentially, we were able to show that the struggle today was between those who sought change within the framework of the Constitution and those who were ready to jettison the terms of the transition to democracy. The report proved to be hugely influential in South Africa, and we think it has played an important role in galvanising political opposition to state capture from constituencies beyond the middle classes. It marked an inflection point in two ways. In the first place, it provided a new vocabulary for understanding political dynamics that was readily taken up in the media and especially among social movements and political organisations, even those allied to the ANC. Terms like 'shadow state', 'silent coup' and 'repurposing institutions' have become part of the everyday language of political discussion about South Africa. Secondly, in concert with a range of university-based institutes and NGOs, the report has been influential in galvanising a new kind of political activism in South Africa – one that focuses on defending honourable civil servants and building progressive state administrations.

The launch of the report on 25 May 2017 was covered live by one of the major national television channels, eNCA. It was all over the radio and there were numerous interviews with the authors. The print media gave the report extensive coverage. It was front-page news in most of South Africa's major daily and weekly publications, and it was the lead story in the Sunday newspapers. *City Press*, for example, South Africa's second-largest weekly paper, reported carefully on the report's argument and on the new terminology it introduced. It also generated numerous opinion pieces in various papers.

The weekend after our report came out an enormous trove of emails, which became known as the #GuptaLeaks, began to trickle into the public domain. The emails have provided, and continue to provide, rich confirmation of our argument. We had discussed the emergence of a 'shadow state', and how political power was seeping away from constitutional bodies. Apart from furnishing evidence of further illegal rent seeking, the leaked emails provide details of Gupta associates' involvement in the day-to-day administration of key government departments – writing speeches, commenting on proposals, suggesting regulations. That is, they are witness to the evolving, silent coup d'état that was taking place.

The reception of our report among political parties was no less spectacular, especially within parts of the ANC and within the SACP. The SACP and the ANC have been long-standing historical allies (since at least the 1950s) and, together with the Congress of South African Trade Unions (Cosatu), form the Tripartite Alliance, the united front that spearheaded resistance to apartheid and that today makes up the political coalition that forms the government of the country. The rise to power of Jacob Zuma is, in part, credited to the SACP and to the unwavering support given to him at the time by its general secretary, Blade Nzimande.

While the SACP had become increasingly critical of the ANC and, especially, of its president, tensions merely smouldered. The report seems to have been the match that set them on fire. The weekend after the launch Blade Nzimande came out strongly to endorse the argument, using the report's terms and concepts. He has continued to do so.

Most dramatically, the country's largest-circulation daily newspaper, *The Star*, reported:

> Due to the damning report, pressure mounted on Nzimande to break his silence on the alleged looting of the public purse by the Guptas. During his party's 14th national congress this week, Nzimande assured his supporters that his relationship with Zuma had broken down irreparably due to the Guptas' influence on the incumbent.[7]

When we were invited to present the report to the SACP's 14th National Congress, the details were received in hushed silence. Apart from the nearly 2 000 delegates, many Cabinet ministers and senior political figures attended. The ANC's deputy secretary general, Jessie Duarte, was heard complaining bitterly to a party official that the SACP had organised a 'hostile' congress.

Since then the SACP has come out officially against state capture and has supported efforts in the ANC to remove the president. In a surprise Cabinet reshuffle in October 2017 Blade Nzimande was dropped from the Cabinet. Then, on Wednesday, 29 November, for the first time in its history the SACP contested a local government election as an independent party against the ANC. This was an unprecedented development that signalled the end of the historical alliance between the two movements.

If this marks the most dramatic consequence of the report, the study has been useful in galvanising action across civil society too. It was widely taken up by some of South Africa's major trade unions. Since at least 1985 the largest unions in South Africa have been affiliated to Cosatu. In April 2017 several Cosatu affiliates left Cosatu to form a new body, the South African Federation of Trade Unions, with Cosatu's former general secretary, Zwelinzima Vavi, as its general secretary. They were joined by the massive National Union of Metalworkers of South Africa, which, three years earlier, had been expelled from Cosatu for its increasingly robust criticism of the union leadership and of the ANC.

When he was still general secretary of Cosatu, Vavi had said that under Jacob Zuma South Africa was headed for a 'predator state'.[8] Whereas this criticism had previously rested on accusations of corruption in the ANC, after May 2017 there was growing appreciation of the relationship between corruption and a disregard for the Constitution and the rule of law.

This is a significant development, especially because, for many involved, there is sympathy for the argument that the 1996 Constitution was the result of an 'elite pact' that came at the expense of workers and the poor. As will become evident below, this had made possible new kinds of unexpected and even awkward political alliances.

The SACC, the largest ecumenical association of Christian churches in the country, was already active in the struggle against corruption. It had convened confessionals for compromised politicians and officials and others with information about corruption to 'unburden themselves'. The SACC hosted a national public event to announce its commitment to opposing state capture a week before we released our report. Many originally believed that *Betrayal of the Promise* was a church document.

We had consulted with the SACC, but our report was compiled completely independently of the 'unburdening panel'. The problem the SACC had was that all those who 'unburdened' did so on condition that their testimony remained confidential. This made it impossible for the SACC to use the information to compile its own report. However, when the SACC read our report it said our analysis accorded exactly with the first-hand testimony it had received from church members across the country, including very high-level officials and politicians.

The church mobilised religious opposition to the Zuma administration. The SACC position was taken up by a group of 'veterans and stalwarts' of the ANC, who addressed an open letter to the secretary general of the organisation, explaining:

> Our hearts are broken as we watch some in the leadership of our movement ... abrogate to themselves the power of the State to serve their own self-interests rather than the interests of the people of South Africa.[9]

In July 2017 the largest gathering of civil society organisations came together under the umbrella of the Future South Africa coalition to fight state capture and to rebuild state integrity.

Business associations were also mobilised. The firing of Nhlanhla Nene galvanised the 'Young Turks' in Business Leadership South Africa (BLSA), who had ousted the old guard collected around the likes of Anglo American's Bobby Godsell. They activated public action by chief executive officers, issued press statements that were openly critical of government and raised funds to support various anti-state capture campaigns, including a public relations campaign to counter the infamous Bell Pottinger campaign funded by the Guptas. Other business coalitions were also activated and a new bilateral dynamic opened up between business and the trade union movement. The BLSA attended an *indaba* on state capture hosted by the SACP.

Two features of this coalition are notable. The first is that, though it comprises many of the people and the kinds of organisations that advanced the anti-apartheid struggle in the 1980s and 1990s, and in this sense marks a revival of an older civil society, it is not exclusively made up of such groupings. Organised business formations have shared a platform with radical trade unionists and avowedly liberal associations.

The second notable feature is that civil society activists in South Africa have, for the first time, taken up issues of state building and, even more surprisingly, of public administration. For the first time there is appreciation of the fact that the immediate victims of tyranny in South Africa have been honest civil servants committed to a public service ethos. The move towards tyranny has, first and foremost, been a political war waged within and for state administrations. This fact goes some way towards explaining why journalists and activists have not been subject to the kind of repression seen elsewhere.

Civil society tactics

All these initiatives taken together saw the re-emergence in 2017 of powerful coalitions of civil society groupings, often bringing together new and unexpected partners. Working separately, and occasionally together, they have used four effective tactics.

Litigation

The growing lawlessness of the government has made litigation an often powerful tool. The High Courts have overwhelmingly safeguarded their independence, and civil society groupings have used them to successfully challenge illegal government decisions and appointments – ranging from challenging the president's appointments of heads of key state institutions (such as the state prosecuting authority and the police) to reinstating criminal charges against Zuma himself, to upholding the independence of state organs, to insisting on the force of law of constitutional principles and to further developing the jurisprudence on public law.

Social mobilisation

Some civil society groupings have successfully drawn people onto the streets in fairly large numbers. Especially important is the fact that they have constituted new and diverse publics willing to speak out against state abuse of power and national resources.

Political mobilisation

Especially impressive has been the ability of activists to build energetic and diverse political coalitions, drawing senior figures in the ANC itself into alliances with a broad range of other organisations.

Unsettling hegemony

The shift to tyranny in South Africa has been accompanied by political arguments about the nature of South Africa's transition from apartheid to democracy, and about the Constitution. Essentially, the Zuma government was able to justify growing criminality as a necessary instrument for radical change, and to depict opponents as acolytes of 'white monopoly capitalism'. Reports like *Betrayal of the Promise* played a key role in unsettling these claims and providing a new language of resistance.

Another country?

From 16 to 20 December 2017 members of the ANC gathered in Johannesburg for the movement's 54th National Conference, at which a new president of the organisation would be elected. Cyril Ramaphosa, the then deputy president of South Africa, defeated Nkosazana Dlamini-Zuma, a candidate strongly affiliated to the networks of tyranny.

The result, however, did not represent a straightforward victory for Ramaphosa and his faction. Former key allies of Jacob Zuma now occupy three of the top six positions in the organisation. In the broader National Executive Committee (NEC), consisting of 80 people, Ramaphosa's supporters comprise 41 members. What distinguishes Ramaphosa from Dlamini-Zuma, apart from questions of policy, is that he is more of a constitutionalist – after all, he was one of the key architects of the Constitution. We will have to see whether he is able to stamp his authority on the party. What is certain, though, is that he and the ANC now operate in a different country, one that is less naïve about risks to democracy and development.

There is fire in the belly of a rejuvenated civil society. The courts have stood by the Constitution, and parts of the media have played heroic roles. In various state administrations and across government numerous officials and public servants have quietly resisted tyranny. Parliament has discovered its authority. In all of this civil society organisations have played a leading role. The publication of the *Betrayal of the Promise* report was a key moment in this process, and reveals the constructively critical role that academics can – and must – play to build frameworks of meaning that help societal actors to make better sense of what is going on.

That said, the challenges that lie ahead cannot be underestimated. Just because the kingpin, Jacob Zuma, has been removed from his position of power at the apex of the structure that holds the constitutional and shadow states together does not mean that the criminal networks have disappeared.

Undoubtedly the power elite centred on the Gupta–Zuma nexus has been critically weakened as a result of Zuma's departure. However, these networks are effective because they are remarkably resilient. They can adapt and morph to meet new circumstances. Much will depend on the effectiveness of the Judicial Commission of Inquiry into State Capture, which will have the right to refer matters to the prosecuting authorities.[10]

However, this assumes that prosecuting authorities are able to act. Actions taken by both the NPA and its Asset Forfeiture Unit against Gupta-linked companies in early 2018 are a healthy sign. Much will depend on whether Cyril Ramaphosa is prepared to act against members of the NEC of the ANC, including those in the so-called 'Top Six' such as Ace Magashule, the secretary general, who have been staunch Zuma supporters and have been implicated in shadow-state networks.

Economic policy will be the greatest challenge facing the government. Rebuilding the state will be no less important. The South African state, unlike the states of South-East Asia (the 'developmental states'), is relatively new, just over a century old. Moreover, for large parts of the 20th century the administrative structure of the country was broken up by the apartheid government. So, by the end of the apartheid era there were 14 separate and parallel administrations, each with its own government and government departments in the Bantustans, together with the racialised administrations of the tricameral system at the national level. For this reason, the ANC's tendency has been to maximise political control of government administrations. This made sense in the early days of the transition when apartheid-era public servants were thought to be incapable of implementing the government's Reconstruction and Development Programme (RDP) initiated shortly after the first democratic election of 1994, and, worse, of being a potential source of counter-revolution.

Hence, far-reaching steps were taken to locate key administrative power within the executive arm of government. At the same time, in the name of the 'new public management' movement that became popular internationally and in South Africa (via the public management schools) during the 1990s, much of government's work has been effectively outsourced to private companies, consultants and contractors.

This combination of politicisation of public administrations and of outsourcing has given state capture its particular form – from manipulating government appointments to directing tenders to selected beneficiaries. Moving beyond the logic of state capture, therefore, requires that we rethink some of the design features of government. How do we professionalise administrations, protect public servants and officials from undue political interference, and bring transparency and reason to public procurement?

It is arguable that South Africa has never had a national consensus on economic policy. The closest it came was the original RDP. However, this was replaced by the Growth, Employment and Redistribution (Gear) policy in 1996 – a policy that was imposed by the then minister of finance with minimal consultation. This policy was later upgraded and renamed the Accelerated and Shared Growth Initiative for South Africa (ASGISA), and included a reference to 'binding constraints'.

In the early 2000s, as the debt-financed consumer boom reached its limits, public-sector funding of national infrastructure emerged as a substitute strategy for growing the economy, underpinning the adoption of 'developmental state' discourse from 2002 onwards. It was followed by the New Growth Path, and the National Development Plan (NDP).[11] The former was driven mainly by the DTI, but with little funding for its central tenet, which was industrial policy. The latter emphasised the need for 'flexible labour markets', an approach vehemently opposed by Cosatu and the SACP.

Despite promises given to the Tripartite Alliance partners by the NDP Commission that the rather weak economic chapter of the NDP would be revisited, this never happened. We now have the 'radical economic transformation' and 'inclusive growth' frameworks, both of which lack any systematic articulation.

During the Mbeki era economic policy tended to emphasise market-oriented strategies coupled to a BEE approach that linked emerging black business to contracts and deals with white business. As we argue in this book, the real economy was being transformed by three forces that undermined investments in the productive economy, namely, financialisation, the shareholder value movement and BEE.

Financialisation was about stimulating economic growth via consumer spending, funded by the expansion of access to debt, by the growing middle class and by the increasingly desperate working class. Shareholder value was about unbundling the conglomerates and increasing returns to shareholders. This resulted in a greater proportion of wealth accruing to shareholders than to labour during the post-1994 era. And finally, BEE resulted in the transfer of wealth from white to black shareholders and managers. Together, financialisation, shareholder value and BEE undermined what South Africa needed most – an increase in investment in the productive economy.

During the Zuma era the focus shifted to the procurement spend of the SOEs as the primary vehicle for building a black industrial class. This had two consequences. Firstly, it reinforced a questionable assumption that capital-intensive investments in large-scale infrastructure lead to the type of growth and development that is needed. Capital-intensive investments, however, have a poor rand-to-job ratio. Secondly, it prepared the way for state capture as the shadow-state networks came to broker the deal-making process.

It is clear that what is needed during the post-Zuma era is an investment-led, job- and livelihood-creating growth strategy that is focused on the building of an inclusive and sustainable economy. What this means in practice needs to be carefully worked out in the course of 2018 and beyond.

It may well entail fiscal expansion beyond what National Treasury has traditionally been comfortable with, and it may require the Reserve Bank to go beyond a narrow focus on inflation when it comes to setting monetary policy. If high interest payments can be offset by the benefits of accelerated and more inclusive growth, a more equitable economy may well be affordable in the medium term. However, everything will depend on whether it will be possible to clean up state administration, re-establish the SOEs as viable public corporations and discipline the private sector, which is focused on short-term capital gains and mechanisms for accelerated investments outside South Africa.

Notes and references

1   Bhorat, H, M Buthelezi, I Chipkin, S Duma, L Mondi, C Peter, M Qobo, M Swilling & H Friedenstein. 2017. *Betrayal of the Promise: How South Africa Is Being Stolen.* Johannesburg: Public Affairs Research Institute.

2   The Right2Know Campaign is a movement that campaigns for freedom of expression and access to information in South Africa. See http://www.r2k.org.za/about/.

3   Ministerial Review Commission on Intelligence. 2008. 'Intelligence in a constitutional democracy'. Available at: cdn.mg.co.za/uploads/final-report-september-2008-615.pdf.

4   Black First Land First defines itself as 'a pan-Africanist and revolutionary socialist political party in South Africa'. See https://blf.org.za/.

5   Republic of South Africa. 1996. *The Constitution of the Republic of South Africa*: Section 217 (1), (2). Pretoria: Republic of South Africa.

6   Public Protector South Africa. 2016. *State of Capture.* Available at: http://cdn.24.co.za/files/Cms/General/d/4666/3f63a8b78d2b495d88f10ed060997f76.pdf.

7   Available at: www.iol.co.za/news/special-features/the-zuma-era/nzimande-dismayed-by-looted-40bn-10300509.

8   Available at: https://www.news24.com/SouthAfrica/Politics/Political-hyenas-in-feeding-frenzy-20100826.

9   Available at: www.dailymaverick.co.za/article/2017-05-25-open-letter-from-the-stalwarts-for-the-sake-of-our-future-take-a-stand-and-defend-our-revolution/#.WiLJ8raB3Vo.

10 The appointment of a Judicial Commission of Inquiry into State Capture was announced by Jacob Zuma in January 2018, following a lengthy legal process challenging the recommendations of the public protector that such a commission should be established. See https://www.timeslive.co.za/politics/2018-01-09-zuma-appoints-commission-of-inquiry-into-state-capture/; https://www.timeslive.co.za/politics/2018-01-25-in-full-state-capture-inquiry-to-probe-guptas-zuma-and-ministers/.

11 Department of Economic Development. 2011. *The New Growth Path*. Pretoria: Department of Economic Development; National Planning Commission. 2012. *National Development Plan 2030: Our future – make it work*. Available at: http://www.gov.za/sites/www.gov.za/files/Executive%20Summary-NDP%202030%20-%20Our%20future%20-%20make%20it%20work.pdf.

1

Structuring the Capture of the State

The nexus between the constitutional and shadow states depends on the integration of a range of skills similar to those present in most international corporations. The composition of the Zuma-centred power elite is, in many respects, highly organised, following the structure of what, in academic terms, is called a 'war economy'.[1] In a war economy the 'shadow state' establishes a number of informal structures which produce systems of 'profit, power and protection'[2] that, in turn, serve to further their operations, making possible continued preferential access to resources and power through an exploitative economic system. The cycle can, therefore, continue.

One of the key requirements in establishing these shadow structures is the ability to secure a system of command and control over the way the resources are accessed, moved and distributed. At the outset, control must be established over the sources of extraction, including the ability to respond flexibly to any changes in the operating environment.[3] Once access to the source of extraction is secured, networks of middlemen or brokers must be established that can move resources externally, usually transnationally, to sustain loyalty (this is critical to ensuring the survival of the network). The ability to transact within this network is facilitated by establishing political marketplaces where support is traded through the provision of access to resources.

The skills of this patronage network are localised within a number of groups. The networks consist of three elements: the controllers, the elites and the entrepreneurs (also known as brokers), as shown in Figure 1.1.

The *controllers*, or patrons, of resources sit at the apex and are usually the strongmen directly responsible for predation and exploitation. Their function is to secure access to and maintain control over resources.[4] A patron or controller typically favours one group over another (or others), resulting in the exclusion of those who are out of favour. This sets up a competitive set of nodes around the patron or controller, which has the ultimate effect of rendering elites (the next layer down) unable to cooperate effectively as they fear being ousted by their partners, or falling out of favour with the patron. Jacob Zuma and the Guptas have been controllers.

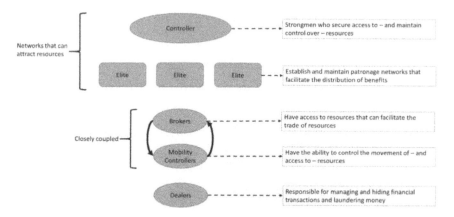

Figure 1.1. *Generalised model of a patronage network that extracts and administers rents*

The *elites* are responsible for establishing and maintaining patronage networks, which facilitate the distribution of benefits. In the South African context the elites would be such players as Free State premier Ace Magashule, ministers Faith Muthambi, Malusi Gigaba and Mosebenzi Zwane, Eskom's Anoj Singh and the ubiquitous Brian Molefe.

The *entrepreneurs*, who are also known as brokers, are middlemen who facilitate the movement of funds, information and/or goods both domestically and across transnational networks, using 'recruitment networks, lending networks, remittance transfers and smuggling networks'.[5] Examples are Transnet's Iqbal Sharma; Eric Wood, CEO of Gupta company Trillian Partners; Gupta associate Salim Essa, a former partner of Sharma; and Ashok Narayan, former managing director of the Guptas' Sahara Computers.

Networks of *brokers* secure domestic and cross-border operations through which resources can be moved to international clearing hubs and enter legitimate trade activities. Brokers are often of a different nationality or ethnicity from the controller or patron – usually a minority group – so that they cannot mount a significant challenge. They have commercial ties to different clusters of communities through which they are able to achieve networked competence, and they have access to ports of entry. Brokers and ports are 'choke points' for intervention in patronage networks.[6] If brokers are identified and their ability to operate is significantly reduced, the patronage network is weakened and may collapse.

Dealers are groups that are able to move the money transnationally (for example, the professional money-laundering syndicates in Hong Kong, the United Arab Emirates and elsewhere).[7]

An essential requirement is to secure and establish cross-border networks to move illicit proceeds into international clearing hubs where they enter the legitimate trade and accrue value to the members of the network.[8] In many instances the networks use clandestine methods to mask the origins of resources in order to protect their members from external scrutiny.[9] From an operational perspective, these networks of brokers and dealers must perform a number of functions.

- They collude with customs or corrupt officials to create false records pertaining to the types of goods traded, quantities and the identities of parties involved in the transactions.
- They provide licences for others to obtain illicit goods in violation of the law.
- They launder cash generated from illicit activities in collusion with formal financial institutions in order to establish legitimate business entities that can generate funds.
- They use shell companies in order to hide ownership details and move assets offshore (for example, the Gupta entities Homix, Regiments Asia, Morningstar International, and so on).
- They exchange one potentially traceable commodity, such as oil or timber, for another less traceable one, in a process also known as trade misinvoicing.
- They purchase legitimate goods outside the country with the proceeds of illicit activities, then import the legitimate goods back into the country to generate 'clean revenues'.[10] The R200 million temple the Guptas are building in India and their R448 million villa in Dubai, reportedly the most expensive house in the United Arab Emirates, may fall into this category.

Ultimately, the key to realising the full potential of control over resources is the ability to strip assets and convert them into monetary resources – typically through money laundering – that can fund the patronage operations.[11]

The conversion of such assets also requires the existence of an appropriate infrastructure for handling and moving them. Such infrastructure includes banking and 'alternative remittance systems ... import-export firms that participate in false invoicing schemes, precious metal markets, and the use of trusts, international business companies, and non-transparent jurisdictions as mechanisms to hide funds'.[12]

Money-laundering procedures

Money laundering is the process of transforming illicit money into ostensibly legitimate assets. It typically follows a three-stage process: placement, layering and integration. Placement involves moving funds into activities or accounts from which they can be legitimised through layering (blending illegitimate with legitimate funds, recycling them through cash-based operations, moving them into 'legitimate companies' or moving them around in complex transactions, and so on). These funds are then integrated back into the revenue stream of the money launderer (often by purchasing property and other goods).

The laundering process usually requires a financial system with lax regulations and controls. Rents are also often distributed in cash and, indeed, this may be preferable in many instances, but there are limits to how beneficiaries can make use of cash in formal transactions because large cash dealings can trigger high-risk alerts with banks. The benefit of cash is that it can be moved overseas, through both formal and informal channels, including the use of diplomatic immunity to traffic large sums of cash across borders (which could raise further questions about the Guptas' apparently preferential access to the Waterkloof Airforce Base) and the use of informal money exchange networks such as the hawala network, a method of transferring money without any actual movement of cash.

The broker network in action: Transnet and Hong Kong transactional flows

With the patronage network model in mind, the Guptas' apparent access to lucrative Transnet work and the subsequent movement of related funds, both domestically and transnationally, is instructive.

Controller/patron and elite stages

Zuma appointed Malusi Gigaba as minister of public enterprises in November 2010, about 18 months after he became president.

Brokers established

Gigaba succeeded in moving Gupta brokers into Transnet, thus enabling Gupta-linked entities to benefit from Transnet tender opportunities. Chapter 2 describes the way in which he did this.

Brokers at work: extracting the resources

Locomotives

While he chaired the Transnet Board's Acquisitions and Disposals Committee, Iqbal Sharma oversaw the adjudication of a R51 billion tender for the purchase of 1 064 locomotives, which was ultimately split among four companies: China North Rail (232 diesel locomotives at R7.8 billion), China South Rail (359 electric locomotives at R14.6 billion), General Electric (233 diesel locomotives at R7.1 billion) and Bombardier (240 electric locomotives at R10.4 billion). Chapter 2 gives details about how the Guptas apparently aggressively represented China South Rail, one of seven bidders then vying to supply the Passenger Rail Agency of South Africa (Prasa) with 600 commuter trains, as documented by former Prasa CEO Lucky Montana.

While, in this instance, they were not successful in their bid to position the rail company, the Chinese company's success in the Transnet locomotives deal appears to have benefited the Guptas. Information seen by the group of researchers who prepared the *Betrayal of the Promise* report suggests that the Chinese company, now called China South Locomotive & Rolling Stock Corporation Limited, following a merger with China North Rail, has been paying large sums of money into Gupta-linked entities based in Hong Kong.

Just before the successful bidders for the locomotives tender were announced, Sharma emerged as a buyer of VR Laser Property, which was in a highly advantageous position to benefit from supplying component parts to the successful bidders in the locomotives deal (who were required by state procurement policy to source a large proportion of their components from South African sub-contractors). In addition, the size of the locomotive deal meant that advice was needed about financial arrangements and corporate structures.

As we will explain in Chapter 2, after a series of highly questionable events a Gupta-linked company, Trillian Asset Management, ultimately benefited from this opportunity to the value of at least R170 million.

Information technology

Chapter 2 details how a national multi-billion-rand telecoms company, Neotel, benefited from significant Transnet work, but seemingly only as a result of an obscure Gupta-linked shell company, Homix, which acted as a broker between Neotel and Transnet. In addition, global software giant SAP was strongly encouraged by Transnet to partner with a Gupta entity, Global Softech Solutions, in order to win Transnet work.

Procurement

Liebherr Africa, a German maker of cranes and a supplier of Transnet, was reportedly pressured by Transnet to partner with Burlington Strategy Advisors, which is a subsidiary of Regiments Capital (see Chapter 2) and which also ultimately paid money into Homix.

Brokers at work: moving the resources

In July 2015 amaBhungane presented the first detailed analysis of how the Guptas allegedly laundered the proceeds of their business activities in an operation that centred on Homix.[13]

This pattern displays the three classic money-laundering characteristics of placement, layering and integration described above.

In moving their money transnationally the Guptas appear to have made extensive use of Hong Kong, which is infamous as a money-laundering capital and where, in the 1960s, 1970s and 1980s, money launderers and couriers made a living out of providing access to underground financial services. While regulations have been significantly tightened, professional money-laundering networks remain active in the country.

The Guptas' movement of their money through Hong Kong is likely to prove to be only a subset of the full extent of their transnational organisation and movement

Table 1.1. Known outflows from Gupta-linked companies and individuals

Dates	From	Destination	US$ (million)	R (million)
December 2012–May 2016	Gupta-linked South African entities	Gupta family members and Gupta-linked entities	Approx. 485.7	Approx. 6 800.0
Late 2014– early 2015	Homix (see Chapter 3)	Bapu Trading (R186 million)	Approx. 13.57	Approx. 190.0
May 2015	Homix (see Chapter 3)	Morningstar (R66–R14 million)	Approx. 3.71	Approx. 52.0
June 2015– December 2017	Homix, Tequesta, Morningstar and Regiments Asia	A group of Hong Kong companies	Approx. 3 370.0	Approx. 4 900.00

of rents. The Gupta-linked companies that feature most prominently in the Hong Kong movement of money are Regiments Asia Ltd (unrelated to the South African company Regiments), Tequesta Group Ltd and Morningstar International Trade Ltd, which shares a Hong Kong address with three companies in which Salim Essa is listed as the director: Regiments Asia, Tequesta Group and VR Laser Asia (Table 1.1).

What is most telling about these transactions is that they far outweigh the claims the Gupta family have made about their revenue streams. Generally speaking, there should be some level of parity between inflows to and outflows from Gupta-linked companies, and some level of agreement between declared revenues from the state and actual revenues flowing to Gupta-linked companies. Yet there is little parity to speak of.

For example, according to the *State of Capture* report produced by the former public protector, Thuli Madonsela, Ajay Gupta claimed, in a meeting with then Deputy Minister of Finance Mcebisi Jonas, that the Gupta family had already accrued R6 billion in proceeds from contracts with state agencies and wanted to increase that to R8 billion.[14] The deputy minister told the public protector that at this meeting Ajay Gupta had offered him the position of minister of finance, in exchange for his opening up access to the National Treasury (offering R600 million to be deposited in an account of his choice and R600 000 to be paid immediately). He had rejected the offer.

By the Guptas' own account to the public protector of their business activities and revenues, revenues for 2016 amounted to R2.6 billion.[15] Government contracts, they reported, accounted for only R235 million of their total revenue. This is considerably less than the R6 billion claimed by Ajay Gupta and suggests that additional revenue generation may have been moving through unofficial channels.

Separately, in 2017 the former finance minister, Pravin Gordhan, submitted evidence to the courts obtained from the Financial Intelligence Centre (which monitors illicit flows of finance) that revealed 72 suspicious transactions over the course of 2015 and 2016 related to Gupta-linked accounts.[16] Taken together these reports and actions make a compelling case for asking questions about how much money the Guptas have been earning from the state, how much of this has been declared, and how much is being moved offshore and therefore contributes nothing to the South African economy.

Notes and references

1   Liebenberg, S. 2014. 'A proposed theory of war economies and a supporting policy framework for dismantling war economies in Sub-Saharan Africa': 3. Unpublished doctoral thesis, Nelson Mandela Metropolitan University.

2   Liebenberg. 2014. 'A proposed theory of war economies': 3.

3   Liebenberg. 2014. 'A proposed theory of war economies'.

4   International Peace Information Service. 2002. *Supporting the War Economy in the DRC: European Companies and the Coltan Trade*. Antwerp: International Peace Information Service.

5   Sandoval, G. 2013. 'Shadow transnationalism: Cross-border networks and planning challenges of transnational unauthorized immigrant communities': 1. *Journal of Planning Education and Research* 33(2): 1–18.

6   Liebenberg, S. 2014. 'A proposed theory of war economies'.

7   Le Billion, P. 2008. 'Diamond wars? Conflict diamonds and geographies of resource wars'. *Annals of the Association of American Geographers* 98(2): 345–371.

8   Le Billion. 2008. 'Diamond wars?'

9   Le Billion. 2008. 'Diamond wars?'

10 Winer, J M & T J Roule. 2003. 'Follow the money: Finance of illicit resource extraction'. In I Bannon & P Collier (eds). *Natural Resources and Violent Conflict: Options and Actions*. Washington: World Bank.

11 Winer & Roule. 2003. 'Follow the money'.

12 Winer & Roule. 2003. 'Follow the money': 8.

13 amaBhungane Centre for Investigative Journalism. 2015. '"Kickback" scandal engulfs Transnet'. Available at: https://mg.co.za/article/2015-07-30-kickback-scandal-engulfs-transnet.

14 'Mr Ajay Gupta continued to speak. He disclosed names of "Comrades" they were working with and protecting. He mentioned that collectively as a family, they "made a lot of money from the State" and they wanted to increase the amount from R6 billion to R8 billion and that a bulk of their funds were held in Dubai.' Public Protector South Africa. 2016. *State of Capture*: 94. Available at: http://cdn.24.co.za/files/Cms/General/d/4666/3f63a8b78d2b495d88f10ed060o997f76.pdf.

15 'According to a letter submitted to my office, total revenues from their business activities for the 2016 financial year amounted to R2,6 billion, with government contracts contributing a total of R235 million of the revenues.' Public Protector South Africa. 2016. *State of Capture*: 85.

16 National Treasury. 2017. *Minister of Finance vs Oakbay Investments and Others*. The High Court of South Africa (Gauteng Division, Pretoria), Case Number 80978/16, 14 October 2016. Available at: www.treasury.gov.za/comm_media/press/2017/2017021001%20-%20ARGUMENT%20IN%20THE%20OAKBAY%20MATTER.pdf.

2

The Politics of Betrayal

The dawn of democracy in South Africa in 1994 delivered a promise that united the country. Nelson Mandela, at his inauguration on 10 May 1994, expressed this promise in the clearest terms. Speaking on behalf of the democratically elected ANC-led government, he vowed

> to liberate all our people from the continuing bondage of poverty, deprivation, suffering, gender and other discrimination ... [to] build [a] society in which all South Africans, both black and white, will be able to walk tall, without any fear in their hearts, assured of their inalienable right to human dignity – a rainbow nation at peace with itself and the world.[1]

To deliver on this founding promise the ANC needed to use the state institutions it had inherited from the apartheid era. These institutions included national, provincial and local government administrations, SOEs, the judiciary, Parliament and the executive.

Unsurprisingly, transforming the core administrations and SOEs into vehicles for service delivery and development became a major challenge. Undertaking deep institutional reform in order to overcome the complex legacy of apartheid proved to be a daunting exercise that required extraordinary levels of dedication, technical capacity and a well-defined governance programme.

Although significant progress was made, there is now widespread dissatisfaction across society and within the ANC itself with the performance of these institutions. Whereas the promise of 1994 was to build a state that would serve the public good, the evidence suggests that state institutions are being repurposed to serve the private accumulation interests of a small, powerful elite. The deepening of the corrosive culture of corruption within the state and the efforts to graft a shadow state onto the existing constitutional state have brought the transformation programme to a halt.

It is clear that while the ideological focus of the ANC is 'radical economic transformation', in practice Jacob Zuma's presidency has been aimed at repurposing state institutions to consolidate a Zuma-centred power elite. Whereas the former appears to be a legitimate long-term vision to transform South Africa's economy in order to eradicate poverty and reduce inequality and unemployment, the latter – popularly referred to as state capture – threatens the viability of the state institutions that need to deliver on this long-term vision.

Until recently the decomposition of these state institutions was blamed on corruption, but we must now recognise that the problem goes well beyond this. Corruption normally refers to a condition where public officials pursue private ends using public means. While indeed corruption is widespread at all levels and is undermining development, state capture is a far greater systemic threat. It is akin to a silent coup and must, therefore, be understood as a political project that is given a cover of legitimacy by the vision of radical economic transformation. While it is obvious that the highly unequal South African economy needs to be thoroughly transformed, the task now is to expose and analyse how a Zuma-centred power elite has managed to capture key state institutions to repurpose them in ways that subvert the constitutional and legal framework established after 1994.

We argue that it is now clear that the nature of the state that is emerging – a blend of constitutional and shadow forms – will make it incapable of driving genuine development programmes. The need for radical economic transformation must be rescued from a political project that uses it to mask the narrow ambitions of a power elite that is only really interested in controlling access to rents and retaining political power.

The Cabinet reshuffles of March and October 2017 were confirmation of this silent coup. The March reshuffle was the first to take place without the prior support of the governing party, thereby moving the symbiotic relationship between the constitutional state and the shadow state that had emerged after the ANC national elective conference in Polokwane in 2007 into a new phase. The reappointment of Brian Molefe as CEO of the power utility Eskom in May 2017, in defiance of the ANC, confirms this trend.[2]

The *State of Capture* report produced by then Public Protector Thuli Madonsela, existing and growing empirical evidence (much of it referred to in this book), information from senior ANC members of attempts to bribe them, well-known sophisticated forms of bribery via 'donations' by businesses to the ANC, the perversion of corporate governance norms in SOEs, the resultant slow disintegration of the Tripartite Alliance (the ANC, Cosatu and the SACP) and much else have made it clear that the 2012 NDP's recommendation that South Africa needs to focus relentlessly on building a 'professional public service' and a 'capable state' has been usurped.[3] Instead of the vision of a professional public service and a capable state being realised, a symbiotic relationship has emerged between a constitutional state with clear rules and laws and a shadow state comprising well-organised clientelistic and patronage networks that facilitate corruption and enrich a small power elite. The shadow state feeds off the constitutional state in ways that sap vitality from formal institutions, leaving them empty shells incapable of executing their responsibilities.

What the power elite cannot achieve via the constitutional state it achieves via the shadow state and vice versa. Some senior officials and politicians have participated unwittingly in this project because they are insufficiently aware of how their specific actions contribute to the wider process of systemic betrayal that has, up to now, remained opaque.

The nation needs to realise that the time has come to defend the founding promise of democracy and development by doing all that is necessary to stop the systemic and institutionalised process of betrayal. It is not too late. The 1994 democratic promise remains an achievable goal, but how is it to be attained?

Understanding the political project

Commentators, opposition groups and ordinary South Africans have underestimated Jacob Zuma, not simply because he is more brazen, wily and brutal than they expect, but because they have reduced him to a caricature. They conceive of Zuma and his allies as a criminal network that has captured the state. This approach, which is unfortunately dominant, obscures the existence of a political project at work to repurpose state institutions to suit a constellation of rent-seeking networks that have constructed and now span the symbiotic relationship between the constitutional and shadow states.

In order to achieve this, these networks are pursuing two aims. The first is to drive a transition from traditional BEE, which was premised on the possibility of reforming the white-dominated economy (now depicted as white monopoly capital), to radical economic transformation driven by groups disguised as a black capitalist class independent of white monopoly capital. The second is to drive a transition from acceptance of the constitutional settlement and the 'rules of the game' to a repurposing of state institutions that is achieved, in part, by breaking those rules.

The result is a strategic shift from reforming the economy, which was the focus of the Thabo Mbeki era (1999–2008), to repurposing state institutions (with special reference to procurement and SOEs) as the centrepiece of a new relationship between the constitutional state and the shadow state. We call the first group, those committed to Mbeki's economic agenda, the constitutional transformers, and the second group working to repurpose state institutions the radical reformers.

The 'Polokwane moment'

Scholarly literature on South Africa's transition notes that the betrayal of the democratic process started early on. The jettisoning of the RDP in 1996 in favour of the Gear strategy marked a profound shift away from a model that sought to reconcile participatory democracy with state-led development, to a model that sought to finance the provision of welfare from a growing capitalist economy.

The first drew on an impressive tradition of radical politics and scholarship showing the complicity of the capitalist sector in the emergence of apartheid. The second married welfarism, market-oriented policies and the racial transformation of economic ownership and control. The first was deeply sceptical of the ability of the capitalist sector, even in a growing economy, to generate developmental outcomes. The second was a bet that it could.

Developmental welfarism started during the Mandela presidency (1994–1999), though its specific institutional form took shape during the Mbeki era. It was organised around three policy platforms and an organisational shift. The first of these was a massive expansion of the grants system for the poor and the unemployed, focusing principally on mothers and the aged; the second, a strong focus on 'deracialising' control of the economy through affirmative action policies designed to fast-track the placement of black people in management and senior management positions; and the third, the transformation of white ownership of the economy through BEE policies.

Mbeki's fourth innovation was the shift of political control away from the ANC itself to the presidency, an institution he sought to build into a powerful apparatus of control and coordination at the centre of the state in order to create a South African version of the developmental state.

The 2007 'Polokwane moment', when Mbeki was unseated as president of the ANC at the 52nd ANC National Conference, is often said to be the revenge of Luthuli House (ANC headquarters) against Mbeki's attempts to centralise government under his control. The party re-established control of the state by recalling Mbeki, the sitting president, and installing a temporary replacement until the conditions were in place for Zuma to become president of both the party and the country. Reflecting his commitment to the party, in his final address to the conference, Zuma noted that 'ANC branches are supreme'.[4]

There were three reasons for the ANC's move against Mbeki. The party, and particularly provincial party bosses, resented the shift in power from Luthuli House to the presidency; black business wanted more state support and was unhappy with an approach that hitched their accumulation potential to the commitments of white business; and radical factions within the party resented the limited nature of state intervention in business matters.

During his years as president Mbeki had engaged CEOs via 'working groups'. Zuma's election created the conditions that resulted in the rise of the SOEs and preferential procurement as the primary means of creating a powerful black business class. At first this was welcomed by the radical factions, who interpreted it as a commitment to enhanced state intervention. The move against Mbeki at the Polokwane conference was based on a conviction about the nature of economic change in a society where the African majority remained subordinated to white interests.

An Africanist conviction

At least since its first national consultative conference held in Morogoro, Tanzania, in 1969, the ANC's position has been that the anti-apartheid struggle was a nationalist struggle led by the working class. The movement said then that 'the main content of the present stage of the South African revolution is the national liberation of the largest and most oppressed group – the African people'.[5] In the 1969 text this was a strategic consideration, tempered by the fact that if the mass of the African people could deliver political freedom it was the increasingly organised working class that would deliver economic freedom. The relationship between these 'phases' of the 'national democratic revolution' has defined the terms of political struggle within the ANC and its alliance with Cosatu and the SACP ever since.

There were signs of a shift in policy at the 1985 ANC conference in Kabwe, Zambia. For all its analysis of the South African 'social formation' as capitalist and its identification of the 'ruling class' as made up of white monopoly capitalists, there was no mention of the working class as a force for change. In the decades since then, the ANC has struggled with the question of who the 'motive forces' of the national democratic revolution are – the working class or the African people in general? During Mbeki's era the answer was the latter, as he made clear in his famous 'I am an African' speech.[6] The challenge faced by the ANC government, however, was that it was neither Africans as a whole nor the working class as such that benefited most during the post-1994 period.

Despite the economy growing at a rate faster than anything seen in South Africa since the 1960s due to the economic policies promoted by Mbeki, black ownership of the economy remained unremarkable. Mbeki noted this in his speech at the Polokwane conference:

> Black ownership of the economy as a whole remains very low; a recent survey put black ownership of the economy at about 12 percent ... If we take foreign ownership of South African-based firms into account, black ownership might be about 15 or 18 percent of local ownership. While we are progressing, our rate of progress is unacceptably low, and we cannot take our eyes off the empowerment challenge.[7]

The problem was not simply the slow pace of change. The 'Polokwane moment' was informed by a basic conviction that the economy remained in white hands and that because of this the 'people' did not share in the wealth of the country. When, in 2010, Julius Malema, then leader of the ANC Youth League (ANCYL), announced the slogan 'Economic freedom in our lifetime', an echo of an older ANC slogan from the 1940s, he insisted on the promise of the Freedom Charter. 'Simply put,' he explained, 'economic freedom in our lifetime means that all the economic clauses of the Freedom Charter should be realised to the fullest.'[8]

The problem with BEE until at least 2007 was that white businesses – referred to as 'white monopoly capital' in government discourse since 2014 – could play within the rules of the policy while at the same time defeating its purpose by 'fronting' – the practice of either appointing blacks to positions without decision-making authority or bringing in 'empowerment partners' on terms that did not alter the balance of economic power in companies. In other words, the BEE route to transformation left white monopoly capital intact. Moreover, it produced a small black elite, while leaving ordinary people, especially women and youth, excluded from the economy.

What was the alternative?

When Julius Malema was expelled from the ANC in 2012 and formed the Economic Freedom Fighters he expressed the alternative to BEE in terms of the need for land and for nationalisation of the mines. Yet within the ANC another strategy was beginning to emerge.

It was based on the simple conviction that the economy would only be transformed to the extent that the grip of white monopoly capitalism was broken and black people owned and controlled large-scale companies. The draft declaration of the ANC after its 53rd National Conference, held in Mangaung in 2012, set the stage for what was to emerge:

> We are boldly entering the second phase of the transition from apartheid colonialism to a national democratic society. This phase will be characterised by decisive action to effect economic transformation and democratic consolidation, critical both to improve the quality of life of all South Africans and to promote nation-building and social cohesion.[9]

The Mangaung conference was preceded by the splitting of the Black Business Council (BBC) from Business Unity South Africa in 2012, because it argued that its interests were not well represented in that organisation. After the split the BBC became the preferred business partner of government. The name of the council is misleading, because it is a professional umbrella institution representing the Black Management Forum, the Association of Black Chartered Accountants, the Black Lawyers Association and the Association of Black Securities and Investment Professionals. Michael Spicer, former CEO of Business Leadership South Africa, contends that although the government formally regretted the rupture, through its funding and other material support it was happy to support an exclusively black business organisation. The BBC also assumed a higher-profile role in the delegations of business people taken on President Zuma's international travels.[10]

The National Empowerment Fund was used to fund the BBC in 2012 with a R3 million grant to promote BEE. The support was intended to provide an alternative voice to what was perceived by government as a historically marginalised group. The DTI provided support amounting to R7 million for similar purposes. The first expression of the Mangaung resolution came in an announcement made by the DTI in 2014, after the BBC had lobbied Zuma. Discussing a new programme of radical economic transformation, the DTI declared it would 'create a hundred Black industrialists in the next three years', further stating that

> over the next five years, a host of working opportunities will become available to South Africans. For example, a new generation of Black industrialists will be driving the re-industrialisation of our economy. Local procurement and increased domestic production will be at the heart of efforts to transform our economy, and will be buoyed by a *government undertaking to buy 75% of goods and services from South African producers.*[11]

As we will discuss further in Chapter 3, the centrepiece of the strategy was to use the state's procurement spend to bring about radical economic transformation. This was not nationalisation but the creation of a new black-owned economy.

The battleground for economic transformation was shifting away from the economy itself to the state and, specifically, to SOEs that outsourced massive industrial contracts to private-sector service providers. Enter Eskom, Transnet, South African Airways (SAA), Prasa and other SOEs, as vehicles for change. This model required preferential procurement from black-owned companies and the displacement of white-managed and -owned businesses from SOE-linked value chains.

The problem, however, was that the existing constitutional and legislative environment constrained this model of economic transformation by insisting that bidders for state contracts satisfy more than racial conditions. Price and experience were also considerations. In other words, the blackness of firms was not a sufficient condition for their securing contracts from the state. Moreover, given that white-managed and -owned businesses had more experience than emerging black companies, were better capitalised and could bring in empowerment partners to circumvent racial conditions, it seemed that the formal rules of the game were rigged in favour of white monopoly capitalists and against black-owned businesses.

This model of economic transformation has been articulated more clearly both theoretically and politically since then. The ANC's policy discussion paper circulated to branches in 2017 was titled 'Employment Creation, Economic Growth and Structural Change'. The document uses the resolution from the 53rd National Conference and the NDP, cited above, as a point of departure for defining radical economic transformation.

> Primarily, radical economic transformation is about fundamentally changing the structure of South Africa's economy from an exploitative exporter of raw materials, to one which is based on beneficiation and manufacturing, in which our people's full potential can be realized. In addition to ensuring increased economic participation by black people in the commanding heights of the economy, radical economic transformation must have a mass character. A clear objective of radical economic transformation must be to reduce racial, gender and class inequalities in South Africa through ensuring more equity with regards to incomes, ownership of assets and access to economic opportunities. An effective democratic developmental state and efficiently run public services and public companies are necessary instruments for widening the reach of radical economic transformation enabling the process to touch the lives of ordinary people.[12]

It is hard to disagree with the ambitious content of this vision. As an ideology it has very broad appeal because of South Africa's economic challenges.

The ideology, however, can also cement a coalition that (largely unwittingly) enables the betrayal of the vision by a power elite that is only interested in rent seeking and political survival and is, where necessary, prepared to use extra-constitutional and unlawful means to achieve its goals.

Understanding rents and rent seeking

Since 1994 the South African government has adopted a wide range of policies that actively seek to reallocate resources across an array of sectors. These include housing subsidies, social grants, incentives for new black-owned industries, BEE strategies, preferential procurement, investment in education, land reform and tariffs.

Neoclassical economists, who focus on supply and demand to determine goods, outputs and income distribution, believe these expenditures are rents that require state intervention and are usually inefficient – a windfall gain for a private actor is a loss for society. Although this perspective is no longer influential it has translated in the past into policy advice about how to 'level the playing field' and ensure 'good governance' by minimising state intervention in order to remove the conditions for rent seeking.

Those whose thinking ventures beyond mainstream or orthodox schools of economic thought believe these kinds of beneficial rents are necessary during certain stages of development. State interventions such as using procurement to benefit certain groups, promoting research and development to create competitive sectors, protecting certain industries during the early phases of their development, favouring historically disadvantaged groups in various ways or subsidising certain actors/groups while they are establishing themselves are all deemed to be necessary if the goal is growth, development and poverty eradication.

Economics literature refers to both productive and unproductive rent seeking. The former (beneficial rents) seeks to achieve clearly defined transformation goals and there is an exit plan. The latter becomes permanently captured by interest groups who use their political power to hold onto rents even when they no longer perform productively.

Comprehending rents and the competition to control rent seeking is key to understanding the contemporary political crisis. What started off, according to our findings, as collusion in relatively low-level corruption between the Zuma family and the Guptas has evolved into state capture and the repurposing of state institutions. In less than a decade the Zuma and Gupta families have managed to position themselves as a tight partnership that coordinates a power elite which aims to manage the rent seeking that binds the symbiotically connected constitutional and shadow states.

What unites this power elite is an ideological commitment to building a black business class, using state institutions to drive investment and growth, and streamlining, through centralisation, the control of rent seeking. Different constituencies are attracted to different components of this political project, from those who simply want to be awarded SOE contracts to radicals pleased with more state intervention; from party loyalists terrified about electoral losses if the economy does not improve to a vast network of people who exchange loyalty for patronage. The resolutions of the 53rd National Conference and the 2017 ANC policy discussion document cited above capture this common purpose. But in reality they contradict what the Zuma-centred power elite does in practice.

To understand this political project it is necessary to understand the limits of the post-1994 policy framework that Mbeki himself talked about at the Polokwane conference.

From constitutional transformers to radical reformers

A critique of South Africa's transition to democracy has been developing for several years within mainstream ANC thinking (originating in the ANCYL under Malema). It has focused on the profound continuities between the apartheid and the post-apartheid economies: the existence of glaring inequality that still largely coincides with the country's traditional racial profile. What is new about this critique is that it increasingly presents South Africa's constitutional settlement as an obstacle to radical economic transformation. This has led to the current clash between radical reformers and constitutional transformers. The former want to subvert and bypass constitutionally entrenched institutions to manage rents on behalf of a power elite, while the latter seek to build state capacity to deliver on the 1994 promise of equality and development by managing rents to promote investment and service delivery.

The difference between radical reformers and constitutional transformers lies in how the transition to democracy is understood. The institutions produced by transition are associated with two different ways of doing politics. The constitutional transformers operate within the confines of the Constitution and are invested in institution building. That is, they believe that social and political transformation depends on giving flesh to the socio-economic rights defined in the Constitution, by building state administrations able to work programmatically to achieve progressive policy outcomes. Their aim is to build a capable state and limit corruption wherever possible. There has been much activism by social movements on this front to force municipalities and national and provincial departments to implement their own policies and to comply with constitutional mandates. The Socio-Economic Rights Institute and the Social Justice Coalition, for example, have used constitutional provisions to win struggles waged by poor communities.

Starting as a revolt against Thabo Mbeki, though not yet associated with a clear ideology, the 'Polokwane moment' gave rise to a new power elite that found a language of its own in the narratives of the radical reformers. Its protagonists claimed to speak for 'ordinary people', those who are not well educated, who do not speak English well, who live in shacks or small towns and rural areas and who are excluded from the economy and the formal institutions of the state. They constitute a politics profoundly mistrustful of the formal 'rules of the game', whether of the Constitution or of government. The formal rules are rigged, this position proclaims, in favour of whites and urban elites and against ordinary people. Radical economic transformation is thus presented as a programme that must frequently break the rules – even those of the Constitution. The argument is compelling at first glance, especially because unemployment and poverty are presented as overwhelmingly black experiences.

The constitutional transformers

For those progressive forces that negotiated the democratic breakthrough and for the many people who moved into government after 1994, the Constitution, which was based on a complex negotiated settlement, was deemed a framework through which transformation could be achieved.

The settlement included a deal made with major conglomerates that they would mobilise investment in the post-apartheid economy – in particular, in man-ufacturing – to support the democratic project. At the time a handful of people representing the conglomerates that owned the large bulk of assets could make this deal. However, the impacts of the shareholder value movement, financialisa-tion, trade liberalisation (from the General Agreement on Tariffs and Trades to the World Trade Organisation), BEE deals and import dependency combined to break up these conglomerates and severely limit investment, particularly in the manufac-turing sector.

Strategic refocusing (as required by the shareholder value movement) resulted in a massive increase in returns to shareholders that, in turn, undermined reinvest-ment (a total of R384 billion between 1999 and 2009, equal to 17 per cent of gross fixed investment during this same period).[13] This was reinforced by transfers to BEE groups (R317 billion between 2000 and 2014, equal to 8 per cent of gross fixed investment).[14] These two sets of transfers (both underestimated here because they exclude transfers to external shareholders and are only for specific periods) created disincentives for reinvestment because of the need to service the (often debt-based) equity claims of these groups.

Debt-based buyouts of key South African manufacturers (such as the South African Iron and Steel Corporation, Dorbyl and Scaw) by local and international companies limited investment in expansion because of the need to service com-pany debt.[15] Furthermore, international listings of South African companies pro-moted disinvestment rather than supporting the much-promised raising of capital for inward investment. And debt-based expansion of consumption to deracialise the middle class resulted in consumer- rather than production-based growth (which had largely reached its limits by the early 2000s).[16]

As a result, South Africa has continued to lag behind its emerging market peer group in terms of investment expenditure as a share of gross domestic product. Data for 2012, for example, show that in China and India investment levels were between 1.8 and 2.8 times those of South Africa. Yet the interesting anomaly is that the rates of return on investment in South Africa are not low; real returns averaged around 15 per cent between 1994 and 2008, while nominal returns were 22 per cent between 2005 and 2008.[17] These rates of return are the same as those of China, albeit over a longer period.

Usually investment levels are high if returns on investment are high. Not so in South Africa. What this must suggest is that non-price factors have affected the level of investment. These would range from product and factor market distortions to structural concerns about political stability and governance. The rate of return, therefore, is not the only factor that guides and influences investment levels in an economy. Furthermore, and exacerbating the problem, South Africa's notoriously low savings levels (fuelling its consumption-driven economic growth trajectory) mean that the country relies on short-term capital flows to finance domestic investment. The dependence on short- to medium-term capital inflows tends to perpetuate dependence on the resource sector, processors of resources and powerful, publicly quoted oligopolies in the services sector. The market power of these companies produces the generous margins that portfolio investors seek.[18]

The path dependency in this job-starved, capital-intensive growth trajectory is starkly evident. The most significant result of this economic conundrum is that poverty, when measured using the official national poverty line (as updated in 2011), increased from 31 per cent in 1995 to at least 36 per cent in 2011.[19]

Instead of using the post-1994 moment to attack the unproductive structure of the economy (in particular the minerals-energy complex), the constitutional transformers adopted economic policies that were inappropriate to direct the restructuring of the extractive institutions at the centre of corporate South Africa. They assumed that a remarkably simple mix of economic policies would provide the framework for macroeconomic stabilisation and growth of a market-driven economy. These included inflation and public expenditure controls; removal of market 'distortions' such as tariffs, capital controls, excessive labour market protections and requirements to lend to particular sectors (to avoid inefficient rents); and a faith in foreign direct investment and the associated transfers of technology and management efficiencies.[20]

This economic cocktail was coupled with an equally simple equation of development with fiscal policy, resulting in a massive expansion in expenditure on welfare, housing, health and education.[21] The combination of market-oriented macroeconomic stabilisation and development-as-welfarism did not adequately address the problem and the consequences of low investment levels, caused by the way the South African corporate structure was being transformed by a combination of shareholder value, BEE deals and financialisation.[22]

Critics of the post-1994 market-oriented economic policies argued that international evidence shows that public investment does not, in fact, displace private investment; instead, it catalyses private investment. Furthermore, international experience shows that lowering tariffs without restructuring by using industrial policy has proven unviable in other contexts (especially where developmental rent management has worked well). These critics further argued that capital account stability was a good thing; that a stable, well-paid workforce was preferable to an over-indebted, under-employed, poorly paid workforce; and that the state needed to lead corporate restructuring actively to ensure that investment rather than dividends and rents was prioritised.[23]

Although the adoption of developmental state discourse in the early 2000s marked a realisation that the state needed to play a stronger leadership role in the economy, this entailed a narrow focus on infrastructure-led growth to draw in private investors, rather than on strategies to guide corporate restructuring and private-sector investment in strategic industrial sectors.

When Mbeki was forced to resign as president of South Africa the ANC was facing the consequences of growing inequality, persistent poverty and remarkably high unemployment levels. This prompted the ANCYL to lead the way in calling for more radical economic transformation. All talk of privatising SOEs fell away, as they came to be viewed as key instruments for ratcheting up investment levels in the wake of the ongoing failure of the corporate sector to adopt a long-term, dividend-oriented approach to investment. At the same time there was growing dissatisfaction in the black business sector; the slow pace of accumulation in this sector was blamed on an over-dependence on the white corporate sector.

The radical reformers

Zuma's rise can be understood in this context. With an economic environment set by the developmental state discourse, infrastructure-led growth, BEE, the emerging significance of the SOEs and state-investment institutions like the Public Investment Corporation, conditions were ripe for an assertive power elite to repurpose state institutions in the name of addressing the contradictions of the Mbeki era. As we will discuss in Chapter 4, the solution chosen by the Zuma faction was heavy dependence on the use of the procurement systems of the SOEs.

Repurposing the SOEs to become the primary mechanisms for rent seeking at the interface between the constitutional and shadow states became the strategic focus of the power elite that formed around Zuma. To facilitate this they needed brokers to help bypass regulatory controls and shift money around (through local and international financial institutions), to finance deals and to transform the ANC into a compliant legitimating political machine. The Gupta networks emerged as the anointed brokers of this expanding rent-seeking system.

Repurposing the state

The politics of radical economic transformation is not focused on the economy but on the state. This was most clearly expressed at the launch of the National Macro Organisation of State Project (NMOS) on 4 June 2014, in a workshop attended by all national government departments. The NMOS was established to implement the new Cabinet portfolios announced on 25 May 2014, after the general election.

Significantly, the NMOS steering committee, comprising all directors general and chaired by the director general in the Presidency, reports directly to the president. The Department of Public Service and Administration acted as the secretariat of the NMOS team, which reported to the steering committee. The NMOS was ostensibly about the renaming of some departments (for example, the Department of Water Affairs became the Department of Water and Sanitation), the splitting of existing departments (for example, the Department of Women was created from the Department of Social Development), the creation of new departments (such as the Department of Small Business Development), the transfer of functions from one department to another, and the reorganisation of departments (especially those that had received new functions).

The 2014 NMOS built on and reinforced the 2009 NMOS, which had initiated the proliferation of Cabinet portfolios. However, there was a renewed urgency in 2014, with the Government Communication and Information System insisting in its communication strategy that 'the reconfiguration of Cabinet and government departments is meant to create a *capable state* that will be able to implement the National Development Plan, respond to the current challenges and *speed up service delivery* to improve the lives of all people who live in South Africa'.[24]

As this statement suggests, the emphasis was on presenting the NMOS as improving service delivery. However, what 'capable' meant and how to 'speed up' service delivery were never further elaborated on. All attention was focused on the operational details, specifically how many departments there were and who was responsible for what. By this point Minister of Public Enterprises Malusi Gigaba, appointed on 1 November 2010, had also taken the first steps towards repurposing the SOEs. Throughout his tenure until 2014 as public enterprises minister, Gigaba engaged in the restructuring of SOE boards, particularly those of Transnet and Eskom, making them broadly representative of the interests of the Gupta brothers and their networks.

Procurement

Meanwhile, along with the ballooning of Cabinet portfolios, the state procurement budget was growing exponentially. In the past 20 years the value of goods and services that government purchases, largely from the private sector, has grown to between R400 and R500 billion a year – testament to the near-complete outsourcing of government's core functions.

Ironically, as government does less there is more and more of it – personnel, ministries, departments, agencies and entities. Essentially, government has become a massive tender-generating machine. The PARI has called it a 'contract state'.[25] This constitutes the core of what could, in theory, be a system for allocating beneficial rents to drive development. In reality it has provided many opportunities for entrenching clientelism and patronage networks that become dependent on the favour of those at the top of the pyramid, who make the decisions.

From this angle the NMOS can be seen as a framework that enabled the knitting together of the relationship between the formalities of bureaucratic governance in the constitutional state and the increasingly significant informal networks of the shadow state, reinforced by the Guptas as external brokers (see Chapter 3) and a parallel set of increasingly compliant intelligence and policing apparatuses (see Chapter 4).

The proliferation since 2009 of government departments at national and provincial levels to extend the political patronage networks has followed the decentralisation of financial accountability to departmental heads (defined as chief accounting officers), which, in turn, was the result of the abolition of the State Tender Board in

2000. The rationale for these financial management reforms came from the new public management movement. Extolling the virtues of 'steering and not rowing', the movement depicted contracting out and decentralisation of financial accountability as institutional reforms for improving the efficiency of the public service. However, lessons from around the world show that combining the decentralisation of financial accountability with a ballooning of the public service creates ideal conditions for a proliferation of corruption. The result in South Africa was the expansion across all levels of government (national, provincial and local) of a competitive kleptocratic culture. By the 2014 election this culture had been in place for more than a decade.

To substantiate this argument we analysed fraud and corruption cases between 2004 and 2016 that relate directly to procurement by state institutions and SOEs (Figure 2.1). A total of 140 cases involved amounts ranging from R70 000 to R2.1 billion. The total amount at stake is a staggering R17 billion. However, some caution is required in understanding this figure. Not all the amounts are known for all the cases, which means the total could be an underestimation. Also, the documentation we reviewed sometimes refers to the contract value and sometimes to the amount that has been fraudulently or corruptly misappropriated. What is significant, though, is that the evidence supports the argument that fraud and corruption proliferated in the ten years leading up to 2014, peaking in 2012.

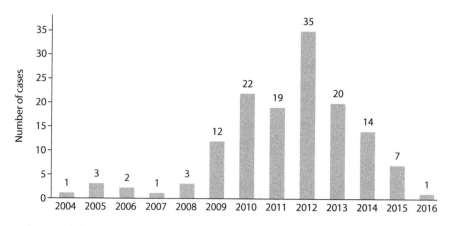

Figure 2.1. Number of fraud and corruption cases related directly to state and SOE procurement (2004–2016)

Table 2.1. Value of fraud and corruption charges against Transnet, Eskom and SASSA (2010–2013)

Region	Date	Particulars of the case	Charges	Amount (R million)
Gauteng	2010	Transnet Johannesburg CAS 2573/08/2010	Fraud and corruption	95.6
Gauteng	2012	Eskom (emergency coal) Gauteng: SEOU enquiry CAS 04/03/2012	Fraud and corruption	121.7
Gauteng	2013	SASSA Payment of Social Grants Net1 Allpay Sunnyside CAS 1274/01/2013	Fraud, corruption and Public Finance Management Act (No. 1 of 1999) transgression	Unknown

Of the 140 cases analysed, only 12 were finalised in court and 62 were still in court in 2017. Sixty cases were still being investigated and nine had been withdrawn, three of them significant: Transnet (R95.6 million), Eskom (R121.7 million) and the South African Social Security Agency (SASSA) (unknown amount) (see Table 2.1).

Signalling that the power elite around him was concerned about increasingly competitive and out-of-control corrupt practices at the lower levels, Zuma instructed then Minister of Finance Pravin Gordhan to lead an initiative to investigate Malema-linked rent-seeking practices in Limpopo in 2012. Although Limpopo accounted for only 10 per cent of the 140 cases analysed, the amounts involved equalled 15 per cent of the total amount for all 140 cases.

Gordhan did more than just investigate, he shut the networks down. The political fallout from this episode (including the repercussions of the expulsion of Malema from the ANCYL earlier that year) in the context of spreading corruption in all provinces led Zuma and other leading national figures to start calling for the re-establishment of the State Tender Board. This reflected a deeper underlying concern, not with rent seeking as such, but with the fact that the extent of rent-seeking competition at the lower levels of the state was out of control (hence the reference in the ANC 2014 Election Manifesto to the need to centralise tenders).[26]

The Limpopo episode may not have triggered, but it certainly reinforced, what appears from the outside to have been a coherent multi-pronged strategy by an increasingly confident power elite to centralise control of rent seeking. In practice, the guiding goal of centralising control was achieved via a mishmash of tactical decisions to exploit opportunities as they came up. The absence of strategic coherence and coordination meant there were many contradictory outcomes, mishaps, miscommunications, fallouts and breakdowns along the way.

With the takeover of the National Treasury made possible by the appointment of Malusi Gigaba as minister of finance in May 2017, centralisation of rent seeking to consolidate the symbiosis between the constitutional and shadow states moved into a new implementation phase. The increased confidence and brazenness of the Gupta networks on SOE boards and in senior management following the Cabinet reshuffle confirms this.

Areas of capture and control

The evolution in recent decades of rent-management systems within neopatrimonial regimes around the world has taken many forms. In summary, though, they can be characterised along a spectrum that ranges from centralised or coordinated to chaotic.

The South African rent-seeking system is a kind of hybrid, partly because of Zuma's personally vulnerable position arising from outstanding and unresolved criminal charges against him; from the Constitutional Court ruling that *he had failed to uphold the Constitution* by flouting a directive from then Public Protector Thuli Madonsela that he pay back public money spent on luxuries, including a swimming pool, added to his rural home at Nkandla; and his embeddedness within a well-structured constitutional order. He aspired to be like Russia's Vladimir Putin or Angola's José Eduardo dos Santos, but was entangled in constitutional state requirements he could not dispense with (like reporting to Parliament and subordination – at least for now – to the Constitutional Court), and in competitive dynamics within the shadow state that the Gupta networks did not always control.

The result was that Zuma, although a powerful political patron, often failed to develop a coherent strategy and was not supported by a powerful professional strategy unit. He was, therefore, committed to a limited set of outcomes that can be summarised as follows:

- securing loyalty across all constitutional and shadow-state networks (including within the Tripartite Alliance);
- enriching his family and the power elite as this recomposes from time to time;
- maintaining the political legacy within the ANC that represented him as a positive force for change, coupled with a succession strategy that ensured he could escape the justice system in perpetuity and continue to exert control over the state through his anointed successor, his former wife, Nkosazana Dlamini-Zuma. This particular strategy failed when Dlamini-Zuma lost the election for ANC president, held in December 2017, to Cyril Ramaphosa.

When the original *Betrayal of the Promise* report was published in early 2017 we could only speculate about how events would unfold. Now we know that these strategies largely failed. The political alliance that sustained Zuma's power in the ANC – the so-called 'Premier League', the alliance among the premiers of the Free State, North West and Mpumalanga – fell apart at the last minute as the premier of Mpumalanga, David Mabuza, changed sides, supporting Cyril Ramaphosa as president of the ANC. An advanced criminal investigation into the Guptas is under way, and Zuma was forced to establish a judicial inquiry into state capture, largely on the terms recommended by Madonsela in her *State of Capture* report.

As Chapter 4 outlines in detail, the Guptas managed to position themselves as the key strategic brokers of the networks that connect the constitutional and shadow states. They began with little more than a tight connection to Zuma himself. Like Schabir Shaik, they turned the political capital of access to the president to their advantage to secure deals in his name, in return for a percentage of the contract.[27] The inclusion of Zuma's twin children in Oakbay companies as early as 2009 was used to full advantage.

For Zuma and others around him it was convenient to have a single clearinghouse where deals were brokered and financial transactions managed at a distance, especially if this clearinghouse was managed by non-South Africans with no loyalties to factions within the ANC. The word in black business circles was that without a deal with the Guptas it was impossible to land a contract with an SOE.

Robert Gumede, of information and communication technology company Gijima, learnt this the hard way when he lost a multi-billion-rand information technology contract with Transnet to the Gupta-connected T-Systems, even though his price was one-third lower than that of T-Systems and his BEE credentials were better. After Malusi Gigaba was appointed minister of finance, this deal was revoked and an attempt was made to reinstate Gumede's bid.

This raises the question of whether there was, in fact, a strategic centre of sorts. In general, the answer is no. Nor was there one single powerful network that overrode all others. The clearest and most disturbing indicator that the South African rent-seeking system tended towards the chaotic end of the spectrum was the collapse of the Cabinet system as the core of the executive branch of the state (see Chapter 4). There is evidence that Zuma tended to govern via a set of 'kitchen cabinets', comprising selected groups from different networks. Kitchen cabinets are small, informal reference groups convened as needed. They can also be shell structures that are activated when needed. As we will show, they have been known to be drawn from the state security establishment, Gupta networks, the SOE sector, sub-groups of Cabinet ministers and deputy ministers, family networks, international networks (for example Angola, and Russian intelligence), key black business groups, the ANC (in particular the 'Premier League') and selected loyalists in the public service (usually loyal directors general).

Kitchen cabinets can be once-off consultative events (such as events involving black business), or semi-permanent structures like inter-ministerial committees comprising people from different sectors and environments formed to tackle a common issue, or regular meetings with key networks (for example, the Guptas or family networks). They are essentially the way the competing nodes within the power elite coalesce and disperse to influence decision-making. Given that it was well known that those with the greatest influence were those who had most recently spoken to Zuma, it is unsurprising that these kitchen cabinets would lobby hard for face-time and follow-through on the deals they wanted to see realised.

When we refer in this book to the power elite, it is essentially to key individuals located in these networks who are united by a sense that they have a historic mission to ensure the emergence of a black business class powerful enough to displace the white business class that remains a dominant force in the economy. How this has been reconciled with the growing prominence of Gupta-linked or -owned companies with limited BEE credentials that win key contracts remains something of a mystery.

Centralising control

The Zuma-centred power elite centralised control within seven broad areas (some of which are elaborated on in subsequent chapters). These were SOEs, the public service, rent-seeking activities, the country's fiscal sovereignty, strategic procurement opportunities, the security and intelligence services, and parallel decision-making structures.

The appointment of Gigaba as minister of public enterprises in 2010 marked the start of a systematic process of reconfiguring the boards of SOEs that lasted throughout his tenure until it ended in 2014. In the course of this process he weakened chronically their governance and operational structures and ensured their compliance.

This, however, was only the first step in the repurposing of the SOEs. The second was to exploit the loophole in the Public Finance Management Act (No. 1 of 1999) that made it possible to use the procurement procedures of SOEs to benefit selected contractors who had been sanctioned by the Gupta network. The loophole is that, unlike government departments, SOEs are not required to table their budgets and expenditure plans in Parliament, which means these budgets and plans cannot be scrutinised in the same way as departmental budgets and expenditures. The details of SOE expenditure can, therefore, be hidden from public scrutiny.

Control over the public service was secured by the fact that after the 2014 election the NMOS steering committee reported directly to the president, creating the opportunity to couple political loyalty and responsibility for specific functions and associated budgets with deals to manage procurement effectively so as to control the rent-seeking networks.

Government ministers, acting in concert with private interests, gained access to rent-seeking opportunities by arbitrarily using regulatory instruments or policy decisions to 'shake down' incumbent businesses – including black businesses – and favour particular interests. They did this by forcing them to take certain actions under threat of losing a licence or not winning a contract, or by threatening not to renew a contract. Instead of prioritising job creation and economic growth, decisions were taken for the benefit of a particular company, faction or group. The Tegeta versus Glencore/Exxaro Optimum deal detailed in Chapter 4 is an example. Common practice would be to secure various financial and non-financial commitments from businesspeople before a particular deal could be approved.

The belief of then Finance Minister Pravin Gordhan and the National Treasury in good governance and a level playing field was regarded as an obstacle to this project of centralising the management of rents; hence the establishment, in 2013, of the Office of the Chief Procurement Officer. Treasury, aware of and opposed to the increasingly corrupt and centralised rent-management system that Zuma's power elite was setting up, used the Financial Intelligence Centre to track illicit financial flows in ways that illuminated the workings of the shadow state.

Prior to the Cabinet reshuffle the Financial Intelligence Centre was the only intelligence agency not controlled by the Zuma network. The National Treasury also controlled the Industrial Development Corporation (IDC) and the Public Investment Corporation, which is the second-largest investor on the Johannesburg Stock Exchange.

Zuma's power elite realised that to effectively centralise the control of rent seeking it needed control of the Office of the Chief Procurement Officer, the Financial Intelligence Centre, the Public Investment Corporation and the unique power available to the minister of finance to issue guarantees. This would only be possible if a loyal minister of finance was in place.

Control over strategic procurement opportunities was secured by intentionally weakening key technical institutions and formal executive processes, resulting in the fact that momentous national decisions appeared to be taken on the basis of ad hoc political judgements, without prior consideration of the legal, financial, economic or other public policy implications. Where technical opinions contradicted the plans of vested factional interests they were actively suppressed or excluded from consideration. Processes were constructed in a manner that avoided deliberation over basic facts and critical evidence; an example of this was the nuclear deal, discussed below.

The loyalty of the security and intelligence services was secured by removing key people from these agencies and appointing loyalists who were prepared to use dirty tricks and other means to deal with troublesome individuals, especially if they were key players. The process went hand in hand with securing control of the SOE boards.

A concerted effort was made to undermine collective political institutions in the executive, including Cabinet. Critical decisions were delegated to handpicked groups, masked as inter-ministerial committees, that were able to function without accounting to any other body. Examples include the inter-ministerial committee on banks (purportedly set up to investigate the regulations and legislation that govern the banking industry, but strangely chaired by Minister of Mineral Resources Mosebenzi Zwane), set up after the banks closed the Guptas' bank accounts; the inter-ministerial committee on communication, unusually chaired by the president; and the National Nuclear Energy Executive Coordination Committee (NNEECC), also chaired by the president.

The nature of inter-ministerial committees is that they lack transparency in that they do not report to Parliament (which individual members of Cabinet are required to do), and they are not formulated in legislation (as is the case with formal Cabinet structures).

In addition, a series of political appointments at Cabinet and provincial government levels reinforced the 'Premier League', with Free State Premier Ace Magashule emerging as its de facto leader. The rise of Magashule to chief political confidant of the president, along with rumours that Zuma viewed him as the preferred candidate for vice-president, pointed to the fact that since the 2014 election Zuma had come to depend increasingly on the provincial party machines represented by the 'Premier League'. Magashule's election as secretary general of the ANC – the de facto prime minister – at the elective conference in December 2017 confirmed this trajectory.

The special significance of the nuclear deal

One of Zuma's top priorities was to ensure that the deal he had negotiated with Russia to build new nuclear power plants in South Africa was finalised. Ignoring the obviously important issues that nuclear is the most expensive form of power available, is unaffordable now and will be more unaffordable when built, due to inevitable budget overruns (as is normal with all Russian nuclear projects), what matters is that the deal emerged from the depths of the shadow-state system and that, here again, the Gupta family was involved, clearly assuming the deal would go through as the president wanted it to.

In May 2010 the Guptas, with Jacob Zuma's son, Duduzane, bought Uranium One's Dominion Mine, later named Shiva Uranium, using a loan from the IDC. This and other transactions related to the deal are discussed more fully in Chapter 3.

In 2011 the Cabinet approved the Integrated Resources Plan, a 20-year road map outlining the mix of the country's future electricity generation, which includes

9 600 MW of nuclear power, and Zuma established the NNEECC, a political structure to oversee the nuclear programme.

In 2014 the contract of Nelisiwe Magubane, director general of the Department
of Energy, a trained electrical engineer with more than 15 years' experience, was not
renewed. A year later the position was filled by Thabane Zulu, who had no experience in the energy sector.

In 2015 then Finance Minister Nhlanhla Nene, in a presentation to Cabinet,
stated that the country could not afford nuclear energy. At the same meeting the
Department of Energy submitted a memorandum recommending that nuclear procurement go ahead. Cabinet approved the memorandum and hours later Nene was
fired. A court ruling in 2017 declared the nuclear procurement plan invalid because
the government had failed to follow due process.

To ensure effective support for the nuclear deal, intelligence capabilities had
been boosted that were now interfaced with the Gupta networks that brokered the
shadow-state transactions to pave the way for the nuclear deal. There are allegations
that one set of transactions involved Russian funding for the 2016 local government
elections, which may explain where the ANC managed to find R1 billion for that
campaign.

The nuclear deal is also central to the consolidation of a new framework for
radical economic transformation. If the deal is implemented it will signify the final
consolidation of Zuma's rent-seeking system as the glue that binds the constitutional and shadow states. It is reasonable to assume that the Russians have linked
approval of the deal to major investment initiatives in the future that could be useful in shoring up the support of black business.

It is arguable, therefore, that alternative energy futures are at the heart of
South Africa's political crisis. According to the Council for Scientific and Industrial
Research (CSIR), in 2016 the price of renewable energy was 62c/KwH over the life
cycle, compared to that of coal, which was R1.03–R1.20/KwH and nuclear, which
was R1.30/KwH.[28]

The CSIR estimated that the nuclear energy option could result in an increased
annual cost of R90 billion compared to the cost of renewable energy. There is,
therefore, no economic rationale for building nuclear power plants in South Africa.
Many experts and commentators now argue that the only reason the Zuma-centred
power elite has pushed the nuclear option is that it creates an opportunity to extract
rents on a massive scale, while giving the Russians the strategic advantage they

aim to achieve in building all the world's nuclear power plants. They are currently building plants in 30 countries. As one commentator put it, Russian nuclear plants are a 'combination of an embassy and military base'. To this one can add another advantage: they give Russia financial control of the economy if the financing is done by issuing a sovereign guarantee.

The politicisation of procurement as a means of achieving radical economic transformation frequently results in the subversion of service delivery mandates. Therefore in recent years there have been purges of professional public servants and the repurposing of administrations away from their constitutional and legislative mandates. This politicisation has also opened departments, and especially SOEs, to massive competition and rivalry, not so much about policy as about who gets what tenders.

This weakens and often breaks administrations, which are then unable to deliver services. A vacuum is created that can be filled by transactions that occur within the shadow state. This is especially devastating for working families and for the poor, who are more dependent on government services than the middle class and the rich. Failures in health and education, for example, reproduce historical, racialised patterns of inequality, distracting attention from the economy itself and the inclusive structural transformation that is needed to make it more productive and labour-absorbent.

Development in an unequal society cannot work without the allocation of beneficial rents. What matters is whether or not the rent-management system is corrupted by clientelistic and patronage networks. Once it is corrupted a process sets in that can lead to the hollowing out of the state, endemic conflict and economic collapse, while an elite enriches itself. This cannot be allowed to happen.

Notes and references

1   University of Pennsylvania. n.d. *Inaugural Speech*. Available at: www.africa.upenn.edu/
    Articles_Gen/Inaugural_Speech_17984.html.
2   Molefe had resigned as CEO with effect from January 2017 'in the interests of good
    corporate governance' after the public protector's report revealed his close association

with the Gupta family. He returned to the position in May 2017, but was removed only weeks later on the orders of Public Enterprises Minister Lynne Brown.

3   National Planning Commission. 2012. *National Development Plan 2030: Our future – make it work*; Public Protector South Africa. 2016. *State of Capture*.

4   ANC. 2007. '52nd National Conference closing speech'. Available at: www.anc.org.za/content/52nd-national-conference-closing-speech-anc-president-jacob-zuma.

5   South African History Online. n.d. 'Strategy and tactics statement'. Available at: www.sahistory.org.za/archive/strategy-and-tactics-statement-adopted-anc-morogoro-conference-april-may-1969-abridged.

6   Thabo Mbeki Foundation. 2016. 'I am an African'. Available at: www.mbeki.org/2016/06/01/i-am-an-african-speech-by-president-thabo-mbeki-8-may-1996/.

7   IOL (Independent Online). 2007. 'Mbeki's speech at ANC conference: Part 1'. Available at: www.iol.co.za/news/politics/mbekis-speech-at-anc-conference-part-1-382829.

8   Polity. 2010. 'ANCYL: Malema: Address by the president of the ANCYL, at the 1st National General Council, Midrand'. Available at: www.polity.org.za/article/ancyl-malema-address-by-the-president-of-the-ancyl-at-the-1st-national-general-council-midrand-25082010-2010-08-26.

9   South African History Online. 2017. 'Draft declaration by the ANC'. Available at: www.sahistory.org.za/archive/draft-declaration-anc-20-december-2012-53rd-anc-annual-conference-mangaung.

10 Spicer, M. 2016. 'The business government relationship: What has gone wrong?' *Focus* 78: 3–19.

11 South African Government. 2014. 'The DTI to create 100 black industrialists in next three years'. (emphasis added) Available at: www.gov.za/dti-create-100-black-industrialists-three-years.

12 ANC. 2017. 'Economic transformation discussion document': 2. Available at: www.anc.org.za/sites/default/files/National%20Policy%20Conference%202017%20Economic%20Transformation_1.pdf.

13 Zalk, N. 2016. 'Selling off the family silver: The imperative for productive and jobs-rich investment': 15. *New Agenda* 63: 10–15.

14 Zalk. 2016. 'Selling off the family silver': 15.

15 Zalk. 2016. 'Selling off the family silver'.

16 Khan, F. 2013. 'Poverty, grants, revolution and "real utopias": Society must be defended by any and all means necessary!' *Review of African Political Economy* 40(138): 572–588; Mohamed, S. 2010. 'The state of the South African economy'. In J Daniel, P Naidoo, D Pillay & R Southall (eds). *New South African Review 1: Development or Decline?* Johannesburg: Wits University Press; Swilling, M. 2008. 'Tracking South Africa's elusive developmental state'. *Administratio Publico* 16(1): 11–28.

17 Bhorat, H, A Cassim & A Hirsch. 2014. 'Policy co-ordination and growth traps in a middle-income country setting: The case of South Africa'. Paper commissioned by the

United Nations University World Institute for Development Economics Research and Korea International Cooperation Agency. WIDER Working Paper 2014/155. Cape Town: University of Cape Town.

18 Bhorat, H, A Hirsch, R Kanbur & M Ncube. 2013. 'Economic policy in South Africa past, present, and future'. In H Bhorat, A Hirsch, R Kanbur & M Ncube (eds). *The Oxford Companion to the Economics of South Africa*. Oxford: Oxford University Press.

19 Bhorat, H, K Naidoo, M Oosthuizen & K Pillay. 2015. 'Demographic, employment, and wage trends in South Africa'. WIDER Working Paper Number 141. Helsinki: United Nations University World Institute for Development Economics Research; Budlender, J, M Leibbrandt & I Woolard. 2015. *South African Poverty Lines: A Review and Two New Money-Metric Thresholds*. Cape Town: SALDRU, University of Cape Town.

20 Zalk. 2016. 'Selling off the family silver'.

21 Khan. 2013. 'Poverty, grants, revolution'; Swilling. 2008. 'Tracking South Africa's elusive developmental state'.

22 Mohamed. 2010. 'The state of the South African economy'.

23 Zalk. 2016. 'Selling off the family silver'.

24 Republic of South Africa. 2014. 'Macro-organization of state national communication framework' (emphasis added). Unpublished memo. Pretoria: The Presidency.

25 Public Affairs Research Institute. 2014. *The Contract State: Outsourcing and Decentralisation in Contemporary South Africa*. Johannesburg: Public Affairs Research Institute.

26 Politicsweb. 2014. 'On the ANC's 2014 election manifesto – Jacob Zuma'. Available at: www.politicsweb.co.za/news-and-analysis/on-the-ancs-2014-election-manifesto-jacob-zuma. Another example of an action to shut down lower-level corrupt rent seeking was the 18-month investigation into corruption in the Nelson Mandela Bay Municipality led by Crispian Olver that started in 2015 (Olver, C. 2016. *State Capture at a Local Level – a Case Study of Nelson Mandela Bay*. Johannesburg: Public Affairs Research Institute). This investigation, commissioned by Pravin Gordhan when he was minister of cooperative governance and traditional affairs, was most likely allowed to proceed to a conclusion because the Gupta–Zuma network was not implicated, meaning that it was probably seen as contributing to the reinforcement of the centralisation of control of rent-seeking practices.

27 Shaik, a close associate of Jacob Zuma, was tried and found guilty on two counts of corruption and one count of fraud in 2005, with the judge stating that there was 'overwhelming' evidence of a corrupt relationship between him and then Deputy President Zuma.

28 Council for Scientific and Industrial Research. 2017. 'Electricity scenarios for South Africa: Presentation to the Portfolio Committee on Energy'. Cape Town, 21 February.

3

Power, Authority and Audacity: How the Shadow State Was Built

Uyangithengisa [you are selling me out]. Why did you let her know
that u knew where she [Dudu Myeni, chairperson of SAA] was going.
U will compromise the mission.[1]

According to the amaBhungane Centre for Investigative Journalism, this text
message was sent by Siyabonga Mahlangu, special legal adviser to then Public
Enterprises Minister Malusi Gigaba, to then CEO and chairperson of SAA Vuyisile
Kona, in December 2013.[2] It followed a meeting at the Gupta family's Saxonwold
compound, attended by Mahlangu and Kona, at which Kona was reportedly offered
a R500 000 bribe, seemingly linked to a controversial Airbus fleet deal.

The text, according to amaBhungane, probably referred to a discussion Kona
had with Dudu Myeni subsequent to this meeting; Myeni was appointed chairperson of SAA a week later, and her appointment, it appears, had been discussed at the
Saxonwold meeting. At the time an SAA source, speaking in confidence to amaBhungane, said, 'The "mission" was clearly this contract, all of these contracts.'[3] With
hindsight, it is clear that 'the mission' became a much bigger, more ominous and
carefully orchestrated long-term plan, which would unfold over the next seven-plus
years, culminating in what we now know as the capture of the state.

Nearly three years later, in July 2016, Jacob Zuma, in a speech in isiZulu
that received very little media coverage but which was captured in a YouTube
clip, said:

If it were up to me, and I made the rules, I would ask for six months
as a dictator. You would see wonders, South Africa would be straight.
That's why, if you give me six months, and allow Zuma to be a dictator, you would be amazed. Absolutely. Everything would be straight.
Right now to make a decision you need to consult. You need a resolution, decision, collective petition. Yoh! It's a lot of work![4]

But clearly the necessary work had been done because the shadow state was, by then, fully fledged. Referring to its emergence, Pravin Gordhan said at the press conference after his removal as minister of finance, 'We have failed to join the dots.'

To 'join the dots' it is necessary to start with the emergence of the Gupta network, which has become the lynchpin of the relationship between the constitutional and shadow states.

The family's privileged access to Zuma after he was elected was a form of political capital that was successfully transformed into a vast and powerful network that effectively brokered the process of state capture and the repurposing of a range of state institutions. The family was useful to Zuma because its members were dependent on him and could, therefore, be trusted to manage the transactions he required. They were loyal to him rather than to any ANC faction or established business interest. They were essentially brokers and fixers who could make things happen for the Zuma-centred power elite with maximum deniability and limited culpability.

The broker-cum-fixer role played by the family is, of course, not unique to South Africa. In his doctoral thesis on the role of brokers in war economies in Africa, Dr Sybert Liebenberg, an independent public and development specialist, argues that brokers are often non-nationals and that their primary aim is always to secure access to state resources, which requires at an early stage 'the establishment of a management capability in close proximity to the actual resources'.[5] As 'entrepreneurs or brokers' they facilitate and ultimately seek to control the 'political market place'.[6] In an article published in the *Daily Maverick*, Dr Vashna Jagarnath, a senior lecturer in the Department of History at Rhodes University, wrote:

> When Zuma won the Presidency, the alliance between the President and the Gupta brothers would make both the Gupta family and Zuma's family fabulously wealthy. This wealth did not come from the kind of productive investment that creates jobs, pays taxes and lays the foundation for long-term economic development.[7]

The Gupta family arrives in South Africa

The Guptas, who emigrated from India to South Africa in 1993, were initially known as the power behind computer marketing company Sahara Computers, but have subsequently become notorious for their close friendship with the Zuma family. In the past two decades they have slowly inserted themselves as brokers within South Africa's power networks, but their nimbleness in achieving this could hardly have been predicted, given the obscurity of their past.

According to the *Sunday Times*, the Gupta brothers – Ajay (51), Atul (48) and Rajesh (45) – grew up in a modest apartment block in Rani Bazar, Saharanpur, Uttar Pradesh, 'a dusty, fly-infested city in northern India' nearly 200 kilometres from Delhi.[8] Their father, Shiv Kumar Gupta, who died in 1994, was, according to locals interviewed by the newspaper, comparatively wealthy. He was, for example, one of a handful in the community to own a car. He apparently made a living running five cooperative stores, earning commission on the sale of oil, rice, wheat flour and cornmeal to locals who qualified for government ration cards. He also apparently made money importing spices from Madagascar and Zanzibar through his Delhi-based business, SKG Marketing.[9] According to Jagarnath:

> Uttar Pradesh is known as a notoriously corrupt state in which gangsters frequently double as politicians. Business is regularly conducted through the intersection of gangsterism and politics. To contain the fallout from the acute social costs of these kinds of arrangements, a rapacious political elite, divided along caste lines, has often backed authoritarian and violent forms of far-right populism, often termed fascism. The aim is to turn the working class and poor against vulnerable minorities, especially Muslims, rather than an endemically criminal and predatory political class. Under these conditions a devastating form of hypercapitalism has been able to thrive while rational, democratic and progressive forms of solidarity, discussion and organisation have become increasingly difficult.[10]

In a 2011 interview with the *Sunday Times* Atul Gupta said, 'We are never shy of our background. I am proud of it. We come from families that do not show or expose their business to others. It is considered showing off.'[11] Both Atul and Rajesh obtained bachelor's degrees in science from the JV Jain Degree College in Delhi and, after graduating, all three brothers commuted between Saharanpur and Delhi for about four years to look after SKG Marketing, and settled in the city in the late 1980s.

During this time Atul completed various computer courses and became a computer supervisor at a printing company in Delhi. The family then sent him to China to investigate businesses there, but this did not work out and the family set their sights on Africa. In the *Sunday Times* interview Atul was quoted as saying 'we didn't have much option to invest in China because they only wanted us to buy between 5% and 12% (shares) in the factory, while Ajay wanted management control'.[12]

In 1993 Shiv Kumar sent Atul to South Africa because he believed 'Africa would become the America of the world'.[13] In 1994, according to Atul, his family transferred R1.2 million into an account he had opened in South Africa. With this money he opened Correct Marketing, an import and distribution business selling computers and components.

At about the same time he tried to set up a chain selling shoes imported from India, but struggled to get customers to pay. In about 1996 he sold Liberty Da Trend, the boutique he owned in Johannesburg's Killarney Mall. Atul said, 'I didn't come with money. As and when I requested money, my family transferred the money.'[14] And so, from a modest turnover of R1.4 million in 1994, Correct Marketing's sales rocketed to about R98 million in 1997 – the year its name changed to Sahara Computers – and it was turning over R127 million by 1999. According to Pieter-Louis Myburgh in his book *The Republic of Gupta: A Story of State Capture*, Ajay arrived in South Africa in about 1995 and Rajesh joined the Gupta businesses here in about 1997.[15]

Given this fairly innocuous entry into South Africa, the origins of the Guptas' close relationship with President Jacob Zuma and his family are even more intriguing. It remains unclear precisely how they first inserted themselves into South Africa's political class, but there seems to be consensus that it was through Essop Pahad, former minister in the presidency of Thabo Mbeki, who was formally introduced to Atul during a visit to India with Mbeki in 1996.[16] The meeting was brief and their friendship grew after the Guptas moved to South Africa.[17]

In 2006 Ajay Gupta, on the recommendation of Pahad, was appointed to serve on the International Marketing Council of South Africa (later renamed BrandSA).[18] In 2010 it seems the Gupta family made an early breakthrough with Pahad, funding his magazine *The Thinker* (the magazine is still published but is no longer funded by the Guptas). Pahad also sat on the board of Sahara.

During Mbeki's administration the Guptas apparently spoke of regular visits to the Mbeki family, but it seems that – apart from their relationship with Pahad – they were unable to gain traction. Myburgh's book describes how Atul was included in a confidential consultative business council constituted by Mbeki in about 2006,[19] but the Thabo Mbeki Foundation has distanced the former president from any meaningful association with the Guptas.[20] According to the *Sunday Times* interview, Atul Gupta claimed that they met Zuma 'around 2002, 2003 when he was the guest at one of Sahara's annual functions'.[21]

Jacob Zuma comes to power

Jacob Zuma was elected ANC president at the Polokwane conference in December 2007. In July 2008, Duduzile Zuma, his 26-year-old daughter, was asked to join the board of Sahara Computers (she resigned in 2010). Duduzane, her twin brother, was also taken under the Guptas' wing and joined Sahara, though the date is unclear. The twins were two of Zuma's five children by Kate Mantsho, who committed suicide in 2000. It has been reported that Zuma has always felt particularly concerned about their wellbeing.

By May 2009 the closeness between Zuma and the Guptas was noted in the media when the president personally thanked Atul Gupta in his address at the end of the Twenty20 India Premier League cricket tournament, which Sahara had sponsored.[22] At face value this may have seemed like the courteous thing to do (given the Guptas' sponsorship of the event), but Jagarnath places it in an interesting context. Commenting on a later cricket event, also hosted by the Guptas – a Twenty20 match between South Africa and India at Durban's Moses Mabhida Stadium in January 2011 – Jagarnath writes:

> One of the Guptas' early attempts at giving a positive spin to their personal wealth and power began with an event held at the Moses Mabhida stadium in Durban on January 9, 2011. This event was held after a Pro20 cricket match between South Africa and India. It celebrated the achievements of Indian cricket legend Sachin Tendulkar and South African cricket great Makhaya Ntini. Bollywood, cricket and politics were choreographed into a single spectacle. This event borrowed directly from a model long established in India where a

toxic mix of politics, Bollywood and cricket has been standard practice for many years. Popular film and sport have been corrupted to
produce a politics of spectacle designed to serve the interests of a
reactionary and rotten political class. The Durban event bore all the
hallmarks of this well-established form of political spectacle. Zuma
was placed in a lineage that ran from Gandhi to Mandela and sur-
rounded by Bollywood stars, cricket heroes and shmaltzy shots of
the Guptas' mother. The celebrity, sequins, bad lighting, lip-synch-
ing and bogus interpretations of history were aimed at wooing the
audience into political narcolepsy.[23]

The Guptas used this match as an opportunity to simultaneously host a concert
to mark the launch of their newspaper, *The New Age*, which was founded in June
2010 and published its first edition in December. At the time of the match and concert the media reported: 'Bollywood heavyweights, Shahrukh Khan, Anil Kapoor,
Shahid Kapoor and Priyanka Chopra, will lead a star-studded line-up that will perform in the New Age Friendship Celebration Concert, which brings together leading entertainment stars from South Africa and India.'[24]

Origins of the nuclear deal

In May 2010, exactly a year after the first Gupta-sponsored Twenty20, the media
broke the story that Gupta-owned company Oakbay Resources and Energy,
together with minority shareholders including Duduzane Zuma's BEE vehicle
Mabengela Investments, had bought Toronto-listed Uranium One's Dominion
mine in Klerksdorp for US$37 million (about R280 million). Mabengela
Investments is reportedly jointly controlled by Duduzane Zuma and Gupta
brother Rajesh (Mabengela is named after a hill overlooking Jacob Zuma's
Nkandla homestead).[25]

At the time that Oakbay bought Dominion – later renamed Shiva Uranium –
media speculation was rife that President Zuma had intervened a month earlier, in
April 2010, to extend the tenure of then Public Investment Corporation CEO Brian
Molefe, to facilitate negotiations towards a large investment in the project.[26] The

presidency denied these allegations, saying that the president's son was 'a business-man in his own right' and did not need his father's help.

The interesting thing was that Dominion had been under 'care and mainte-nance' since 2008, with Uranium One chief executive Jean Nortier saying, 'We had to close that chapter; we certainly weren't going to try to bring Dominion back into production – it certainly was going to require too much capital.'[27] Bringing Dominion back to full production was projected to cost far more than the US$37 mil-lion purchase price, according to media reports. At the time of the purchase jour-nalist Brendan Ryan wrote:

> Who in their right mind would buy one of the most notorious dogs in the entire South African mining sector – the failed Dominion Uranium mine – and do it at a time when uranium prices are still depressed? ... It's either the steal of the century – given that devel-opers Uranium One wrote off an investment of $1.8 billion when they shut Dominion down in October 2008 – or it's a classic case of throwing good money after bad.[28]

Unbeknown to Ryan at the time, and certainly evident in retrospect, the Zuma power elite had their sights set on a large-scale nuclear programme that would create a new and lucrative market for uranium. Molefe seems to enter the story at this point, in what may have been his first move to integrate himself into the Zuma group after long being identified as an 'Mbeki man'. Although he denied having a hand in the Guptas' Uranium One deal, there seem to be too many inexplicable coincidences.

The timing is significant. According to amaBhungane, Molefe's last day as CEO of the Public Investment Corporation would have been 12 April 2010, two days before the Dominion transaction was closed. However, his contract was extended for three months, to the reported irritation of senior ANC and Tripartite Alliance officials.[29] At the time the *Sunday Times* reported that Jacob Zuma was 'understood to have phoned a senior official in the finance ministry to ask that Molefe remain in the job'.[30]

According to amaBhungane, company registration documents show that Atul Gupta and Duduzane Zuma took over as directors of the Dominion holding com-pany on 14 April, the day the sale was finalised. If, as alleged in media reports, Molefe was involved in negotiations to commit Public Investment Corporation funding, his departure at that crucial time might have compromised the negotiations. The investment committee rejected the deal as being too risky, but the IDC provided the loan.

Brian Molefe gains his foothold

By March 2011 the *Mail & Guardian* was reporting several anomalies associated with the appointment of Molefe as the new CEO of Transnet, which, according to the newspaper, appeared to have been predetermined.[31] The Gupta family denied reports that they had influenced the selection of Molefe; however, the media provided circumstantial but compelling information to the contrary. According to the media, the advertisement for the position of CEO was published on 26 January 2011 and candidates were given until 1 February 2011 to respond. Then Public Enterprises Minister Malusi Gigaba announced Molefe's appointment on 16 February. Transnet said 63 applications had been received and 9 applicants had been interviewed. The board's corporate governance and nominations committee, chaired by Transnet chairperson Mafika Mkwanazi, apparently handled the process. The *Mail & Guardian* reported that 'a senior executive with knowledge of Transnet board operations said the applications had to be vetted and interviews for busy executives and board members arranged. "Molefe's appointment was miraculously quick," the executive said'.[32]

Transnet's non-executive director and former CEO of DaimlerChrysler, Juergen Schrempp, who had only been appointed a few months earlier, in December 2010, resigned shortly after Molefe's appointment. While he did not comment, the *Sunday Times* reported that he was unhappy about the handling of Molefe's appointment and about the fact that Mkwanazi had submitted three names of candidates to Gigaba without prior board approval.[33]

Interestingly, on 7 December 2010, about three months before his appointment, *The New Age*, without quoting its sources, had written: 'The New Age has it on good authority that Molefe will be appointed CEO by the board.'[34] The paper correctly predicted other appointments to the new Transnet board, including those of Don Mkhwanazi, a Zuma ally and leading advocate of BEE, and Ellen Tshabalala, a former chairperson of the SABC).

The Guptas set their sights on the SOEs

In September 2012 most of the SAA board, led by its former chairperson, ANC stalwart Cheryl Carolus, resigned, apparently over a breakdown in its relationship with Gigaba.[35] Chief Executive Siza Mzimela and some of her key people followed in early October. This period seems to mark the start of the capture of the parastatal.

It appears that a large SAA tender, worth at least R10 billion, was at the root of the conflict. About six months after the resignation of the board questions emerged in the media about a meeting held at the Saxonwold compound of the Gupta family in October 2012 involving the airline's acting CEO, as well as the special adviser to Minister Gigaba.[36]

The *Mail & Guardian* reported at the time that SAA's fleet committee had selected the new Airbus A350 over Boeing's long-haul offering and passed its recommendation on to the SAA board in late August 2012, and that the outgoing board had agreed to the choice.

According to the *Mail & Guardian* article, the new fuel-efficient, long-haul fleet was central to a detailed turnaround plan that Carolus's board had prepared. SAA was struggling, partly because of high fuel costs, and securing the correct aircraft was key to the turnaround strategy. But Gigaba appears to have delayed his support for this strategy, acknowledging that the fleet committee had recommended that the board procure from Airbus, but saying 'the department was concerned that there was no long-term strategy that had been shared with it that informed the fleet renewal programme'.[37] According to the *Mail & Guardian*, the delay meant that SAA lost the production slot it had been offered by Airbus during its bid.

After Carolus left, Gigaba brought Kona back as both acting CEO and board chairperson. According to the *Mail & Guardian*, he attended the October 2012 meeting at the Guptas' Saxonwold house. Also present at the meeting, according to the article, were Rajesh Gupta, Duduzane Zuma and the son of Free State Premier Ace Magashule, Tshepiso (who at one point listed Mabengela as his employer).

According to amaBhungane, at the meeting Rajesh apparently offered to make R100 000 available to Kona and then increased it to R500 000.[38] The news report did not specify what the money was for, but said that Kona had refused the offer and had later spoken to board colleague Dudu Myeni about the meeting.

On 27 November, following this meeting, Mahlangu apparently sent the text message quoted above to Kona. On 8 January 2013 Myeni, who is close to Zuma and chairs his charitable foundation, was made SAA chairperson. On 11 February the SAA board announced the cautionary suspension of Kona as acting CEO pending an investigation into alleged contraventions of financial regulations. On 11 March 2013 Gigaba removed Kona from the board, citing a breakdown in trust.

Both Mahlangu and a spokesperson for the Gupta family told the media that the meeting at the Gupta residence was about how various companies that the Gupta family controlled could switch their corporate travel business to SAA, and that nothing unlawful was discussed. AmaBhungane noted that 'given that the Guptas' Oakbay Investments owns just under 5% of SAA's rival Comair, this explanation was barely credible'.[39]

The Passenger Rail Agency of South Africa

In late 2012, in a letter written by then Prasa CEO Lucky Montana to then Prasa board chairperson Sifiso Buthelezi, extraordinary details emerged of how the Gupta family and Duduzane Zuma allegedly planned to capture the parastatal and profit from a R51 billion tender.[40] This letter was only leaked four years later, in 2016, but demonstrates how the Gupta network was brokering political access for commercial gain. It was one of the first early warning signals that something more serious was afoot.

The Guptas, the letter said, represented China South Rail, one of seven companies then bidding to supply Prasa with 600 commuter trains. Such representatives, or facilitators, are often positioned to earn huge 'success fees'. According to Montana's letter, in 'numerous meetings' the Guptas, Duduzane Zuma and their associates had allegedly pressured then Minister of Transport Ben Martins and Montana to favour the rail company. They had also, the letter said, proposed allocating shares to Montana and 'directly, unashamedly and unapologetically demanded' that Martins restructure Prasa's board.

Montana wrote the letter after discovering that the National Department of Transport was preparing a Cabinet memorandum to restructure the board. Montana proposed that he 'negotiate my exit' from Prasa, saying, 'I feel betrayed, in spite of having ... been given assurances by our honourable minister that the restructuring of the Prasa board was not on the cards.' His threat to leave apparently led to further reassurances from Martins, and the board remained unchanged.

Another bidder, France-backed Gibela, was ultimately handed the R51 billion tender in December 2012. According to amaBhungane, the BEE beneficiaries included Dudu Myeni's son, Thalente, whose registered address was the Zuma residence in Forest Town, Johannesburg.[41] The BEE consortium sold out of the deal early on. The question here is whether this was a case where the Zuma elite did not back the Gupta bid. If so, the Prasa tender is an example of competing rent-seeking groups, both with access to Zuma, clashing, leading to one winner.

Lucky Montana was, arguably, tied to one of the groups, and he managed to win Martins over in support of the Gibela bid. As suggested below, the key difference between the two bids was that the Gupta-mediated one with China South Rail would probably have required a hefty payoff to the Guptas as brokers of the deal. The Gibela deal, by contrast, followed the conventional rent-seeking route, that is, selling off the BEE stake after the award is made and paying off whoever needs to be paid after that.

However, this did not stop China South Rail and their Gupta representatives. They appear to have gone from strength to strength at another parastatal, Transnet. There, thanks to their close relationship with Molefe, the rail company won tenders to supply 95 locomotives in 2012 and the largest share of the 1 064 locomotives, worth R51 billion, split between four bidders in 2014 (see below).

It is instructive that the pressure on Montana to favour the Gupta-led consortium started in September 2012, only three months after Zuma appointed Martins as transport minister and two months after Prasa issued the train tender. Montana wrote:

> I have previously reported to the chairman of my attendance of numerous meetings at various periods with the minister of transport, key advisors in the ministry of transport and representatives of the Gupta family. It is in these meetings where I was introduced to representatives of the Gupta family and the son to the president, Mr Duduzane Zuma, and their relationship with one of the bidding companies, China South Railways ... I had taken issue with the representative of the Gupta family over what I considered to be attempts on their part to 'extort' money from [the bidders].[42]

Montana told amaBhungane that he was called to a first meeting at Martins's Pretoria residence as he was about to depart for a transport conference in Germany in the third week of September 2012. There he was introduced to Rajesh Gupta, Duduzane Zuma and an associate. They apparently indicated their general interest in the tender. Montana writes that at the conference bidders approached him to say

> that they are required to pay money on the side, that they are aware that the Prasa AGM [annual general meeting] will be postponed, which truly materialised, and further informed that [the] purpose of the postponement was to allow time for the board of Prasa to be restructured. This will ensure that the requirements of the Gupta family and China South Railways are achieved.[43]

Montana said the bidders had told him that a Gupta associate had met with bidders in Switzerland, telling them, 'We work with Lucky [Montana], we work with Ben Martins [and we have] the support of the president. [If] you don't work with us, you are not going to get this bid.'[44]

Montana said he asked for a meeting at the minister's house on his return, where he 'blasted' Rajesh Gupta and Duduzane Zuma. And he told them the correct route was for China South Rail – whom they said they now formally represented – to 'submit a compliant bid'. He said, 'I thought that was the end of the matter. Unfortunately it was not.'[45]

Before the adjudication process, according to the letter, Rajesh Gupta pressured Montana to include two Gupta nominees among the bid evaluators. Their CVs were delivered by a driver. 'I rejected that,' Montana said. The letter goes on: 'I must also add that the Guptas have presented a plan that I and other people have been allocated shares within CSR [China South Rail], the plan which I rejected contemptuously in the presence of our minister.' The letter refers to a Gupta associate's alleged direct demand that Martins restructure the board: 'I was taken aback and continue to be surprised by the fact that the representative of the said family finds such power, authority and audacity.[46]

According to the letter, on 28 October 2012 then Transport Director General George Mahlalela showed Montana 'a written memorandum for the appointment of a new chairperson and other Prasa directors [that] was being processed for submission to the cabinet'.

The awarding of the tender to the Gibela consortium was just the start of bitter battles over access to rents via Prasa. In 2012 the South Africa Transport and Allied Workers Union triggered an investigation by the public protector, who reported in 2015 that there was evidence that billions had been stolen. A new board, chaired by the ANC's Popo Molefe, was appointed in August 2015 to clean up the SOE, but it was apparently not made aware of the public protector's investigation. Lucky Montana was fired in 2015, in part because Molefe apparently discovered that R80 million from a locomotive contract had been paid to the ANC. Molefe and his board were eventually dismissed by then Minister of Transport Dipuo Peters in 2017, shortly before she herself lost her job. Molefe's board later won a legal battle that resulted in its reinstatement.

The Guptas go provincial

Having gained their foothold in the SOEs, the Guptas turned their sights to the province of the Free State where they appeared to be brokering the patronage network of Premier Ace Magashule, a Zuma loyalist.

In May 2013, according to an amaBhungane investigation, a company called Estina, which was indirectly linked to the Guptas, was given a farm and tens of millions of rands by the Free State provincial government to start a dairy. Magashule had endorsed the project in his State of the Province address in February that year. According to the media investigation, the provincial agriculture department had reportedly already contributed R30 million, which was set to rise to R342 million over 3 years.[47]

There were doubts about Estina's capacity to conduct operations. Its only director, Kamal Vasram, worked in information technology and had no apparent farming background, according to amaBhungane. It subsequently emerged that he was linked to the Guptas.

The provincial Department of Agriculture claimed that Estina and an Indian company, Paras Dairy, were jointly involved and had committed R200 million to the project, but amaBhungane was told by a spokesperson for Paras Dairy, 'We don't do any business in South Africa and we don't have any Estina on our database.'[48]

Deeds records showed that Estina had obtained a 99-year lease on the 4 400 hectare Krynaauwslust farm near Vrede from the department, apparently rent free, according to amaBhungane.

The provincial government, the Gupta family and Vasram all denied Gupta involvement in the project, except for a consulting sub-contract amounting to

R138 000 awarded to Linkway Trading, a Gupta company. However, the amaBhungane investigation strongly suggested that the Guptas were playing an active behind-the-scenes role in the dairy project. As the story unfolded it emerged that the National Treasury, through its dedicated public–private partnership unit, had not approved the dairy project, nor had the Free State provincial government sought the required permission to deal with Estina.

Ultimately a National Treasury investigation found that the dairy project had many irregularities, stating that 'a company without agricultural experience and led by a computer sales manager – flouted treasury rules and was designed to milk provincial government coffers'.[49] One of the investigators told amaBhungane, 'Estina is using government's money to establish a plant, putting cows on land that is given by government rent-free. Now they get to make a fortune off the infrastructure.'

According to documents linked to the investigation and given to amaBhungane, the dairy project appears to have been conceived during a visit to India by senior Free State Department of Agriculture officials and then Agriculture Member of the Executive Council, Mosebenzi Zwane, whose hometown is Vrede. The trip was signed off by Magashule.

In June 2014 the Free State Department of Agriculture announced that it had cancelled its contract with Estina, which had nevertheless done well out of the deal after the province ultimately invested a total of R220 million in the dairy farm. It subsequently emerged that only one per cent of this amount was allocated for its original purpose. The rest was used for the private consumption of the Gupta family. Atul received a cool R10 million. The Free State money paid for a lavish Sun City Gupta family wedding, luxury cars and the family's private jet. In January 2018 the Asset Forfeiture Unit of the NPA seized the farm.

The gift that keeps on giving: the locomotive deal, VR Laser and Trillian

On 17 March 2014, while the media reported that many cattle were dying of disease and starvation on the Free State farm, Transnet released a press statement saying that it had awarded a R51 billion contract for the building of 1 064 locomotives

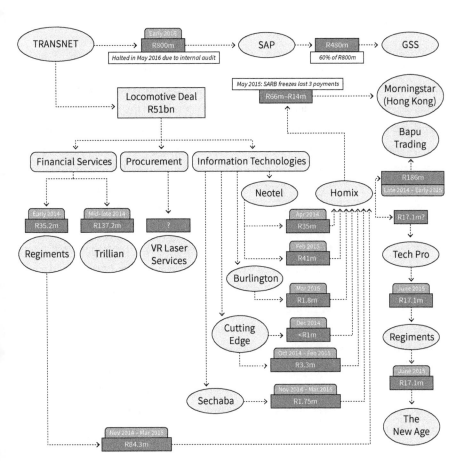

Figure 3.1. Financial flows via the shadow state

(Figure 3.1). It split the contract among four major train builders – China South Rail, Bombardier, General Electric and China North Rail.[50]

The *Mail & Guardian* had reported three weeks earlier that the National Union of Metalworkers of South Africa had submitted a report to the public protector, raising concerns about the way Transnet had structured, adjudicated and awarded this tender.[51] The union contended that government's policy of localisation and job creation had, in the case of the Transnet locomotive tender, been abused by 'the implementation of opaque and underhand business dealings to line the pockets of a selected minority business and political elite'.[52]

VR Laser Services

What piqued the union's and, ultimately, the media's interest in this deal was that the man who oversaw the awarding of the R51 billion tender, Iqbal Sharma, was simultaneously closing a deal which potentially put him (and Duduzane Zuma) in a position to benefit directly from key sub-contracts related to the locomotives deal.

Before his appointment to the Transnet board in December 2010 by then Public Enterprises Minister Gigaba, Sharma had been the head of Trade and Investment South Africa within the DTI. This is where he reportedly met the Guptas.

In 2011 Gigaba had apparently wanted him to be appointed Transnet board chairperson, but the Cabinet vetoed this because he was too close to the Guptas, which signalled that in 2011 Zuma had not yet secured a fully compliant Cabinet. Seemingly to circumvent Cabinet's veto, Transnet would later create a new structure, formally called the Board Acquisitions and Disposals Committee, to supervise the planned pipeline of future large-scale infrastructure spending (comprising all tenders worth more than R2.5 billion). In 2012 Sharma was appointed to chair this committee and it was from this position that he adjudicated the locomotive deal.

In February 2014, a few weeks before Transnet announced the main tender awards, a company in which Sharma, Rajesh Gupta and Duduzane Zuma were partners acquired a stake in VR Laser Services, a Gauteng engineering firm that produces steel plate components for heavy vehicle bodies. Throughout this period Sharma was overseeing the locomotive tender process.

When the story emerged in the media Sharma denied any conflict of interest, claiming that VR Laser did not do – and had no intention of doing – business with Transnet. To distance himself from the allegations, he said he had bought the property company that owns VR Laser's premises, but not VR Laser itself.

However, amaBhungane established that, as Sharma was completing the tender process and the acquisition of the property holding company linked to VR Laser, each of the four multinational train manufacturing companies that would later win a part of the locomotive supply contract visited the engineering company's premises to assess the possibility of sub-contracting work to VR Laser.[53]

The winning bidders for the locomotives deal were required by state procurement policy to source up to 60 per cent of their components from South African sub-contractors, placing VR Laser in a highly advantageous position.

Trillian Group

The size of the locomotive deal meant that financial arrangement and corporate structuring advice was necessary. A Gupta-linked company, Trillian Asset Management, ultimately benefited from this opportunity. The emergence of Trillian, and the company's involvement in this deal, is convoluted but is worth noting because it demonstrates the lengths to which the Guptas and their associates have gone to achieve the capture of state institutions.

In 2012, when Transnet issued the locomotives tender, the rail company appointed a consortium led by international management consulting firm McKinsey to advise on the deal structure and how to fund it. Their consortium partners included Nedbank and McKinsey's long-time empowerment associate, Letsema Consulting. Financial advisory services were included in the mandate and payment was clearly capped at R35.2 million.[54]

Transnet's formal letter of intent noted: 'Any overrun in terms of time will not be for the account of Transnet as the engagement is output based and not time based.'[55] However, these restrictions seem to have quickly been ignored. Months after the contract was awarded, Transnet invoked unexplained conflict of interest concerns relating first to Letsema, then to Nedbank, according to amaBhungane.[56] To resolve this conflict of interest Transnet proposed Regiments Capital as a substitute for Letsema and Nedbank. Regiments, started by six Johannesburg-based entrepreneurs in 2004, is a fund manager and investment advisor specialising in public-sector infrastructure programmes and projects.

At that point Regiments was given an estimated R10 million share of the contract. But, as subsequently became clear, there followed an extraordinary ballooning of the scope and cost of services, driven by then Transnet Chief Financial Officer Anoj Singh and approved by then Transnet CEO Molefe.

In November 2013, following the triggering of the conflict of interest against Letsema, Singh apparently confirmed in writing that the main scope of the engagement would be allocated to Regiments. McKinsey, originally the consortium leader, remained 'only responsible for the business case and limited technical optimisation aspects'.[57] In February 2014 the contract scope for Regiments was amended to reflect a new reality. Although the addendum to the contract purported to be between Transnet and McKinsey, amaBhungane reported that Regiments' director

Eric Wood (who would later emerge as a key Gupta ally) had scratched out McKinsey and signed on behalf of Regiments.

In addition, Singh, signing on behalf of Transnet, increased the contract value by R6 million, bringing the total to R41.2 million, of which a R21 million 'fixed price' would go to Regiments, according to the amaBhungane investigation. Two months later, in April 2014, Singh sent a memo to Molefe in which he motivated for a *post facto* revision in the fee allocation to Regiments, asking to add an additional R78.4 million. The additional fee was apparently based on Regiments' own calculation of 'the billions'[58] its advice had supposedly saved Transnet.

Singh's rationale was that Regiments had apparently demonstrated to Transnet that it could save money by splitting the locomotive order among four bidders (ultimately awarded), rather than choosing one or two. According to Singh, as summarised by amaBhungane, although this would make each locomotive more expensive as bidders would have a smaller volume to dilute their overheads, the full complement of 1 064 could be delivered more quickly. Based on this reasoning, the amendment to the original contract value increased the payment to Regiments from R21 million to R99.5 million. Molefe approved this.

In early 2015 the then group treasurer of Transnet, Mathane Makgatho, resigned unexpectedly. The media reported that she told her staff, 'I arrived here with integrity, and I will leave with my integrity intact.'[59] She was replaced by Phetolo Ramosebudi, the previous group treasurer of SAA, who, weeks after his appointment on 28 April 2015, compiled a proposal purporting to approve a 'contract extension' for Regiments' support to Transnet on the locomotive transaction, raising its fee from the previous R99.5 million by R166 million to total R265.5 million. Without citing any contract Ramosebudi suggested that 'the financial advice and negotiation support that Regiments provided through this entire process, which took in excess of 12 months, was done at risk with an expectation of compensation only on successful completion of the transaction'.[60]

During the course of Regiments' work for Transnet Wood became acquainted with the Guptas, who – seemingly in a bid to get in on the lucrative contract – approached Regiments to buy a majority stake. When the directors of Regiments refused the purchase offer, Trillian Asset Management, which at the time was a small firm of investment professionals owned by four men, including brothers Rowan and Ben Swartz, emerged as a player. Trillian worked with a second investment firm, whose principals included Stanley Shane. Shane, in turn, held two noteworthy board appointments: at Transnet, where he chaired the procurement committee, and at a third investment firm, where his co-directors included Salim Essa, the Gupta associate. According to amaBhungane, he was well placed to make the introductions that followed.

When the Swartz brothers indicated in 2015 that they wanted to sell their 50 per cent share in Trillian, Shane introduced the buyer, a shelf company named Lipshell 103, according to amaBhungane. Trillian's share register shows that the Swartz brothers' shares were transferred to Lipshell on 1 September 2015. Company records show that later that month, in a listing backdated to just before the acquisition, Essa was registered as Lipshell's sole director. Lipshell subsequently increased its stake to a controlling 60 per cent of what became the Trillian group of companies, including the original Trillian Asset Management. Lipshell was renamed Trillian Holdings and Essa remains its only director.

According to amaBhungane, in December 2015 Transnet paid Trillian Asset Management R93.5 million, purportedly for acting as the 'lead arranger' for a R12 billion 'club loan' by a syndicate of 5 banks to help fund the R51 billion purchase of 1 064 new locomotives, notwithstanding the fact that McKinsey had originally been appointed to arrange the corporate and financial structuring for the deal, which then passed to Regiments. Now Trillian was receiving payment for allegedly doing the work.

Usually in such a deal the lead arranger would be one of the lenders – typically an experienced financial or advisory institution, lending at least as much money as each of the others. Trillian Asset Management was a small boutique asset manager, arguably without the capacity to lead a R12 billion bank syndicate. Furthermore, the SOE's own corporate treasury, one of the largest in the country, could have arranged the loan itself. Trillian allegedly did at least R170 million worth of work for Transnet. It remains unclear what kind of work could justify such large payouts of state resources.

On 1 March 2016 Eric Wood left Regiments to join Trillian, and in May 2016 Transnet apparently transferred its contract with Regiments to Trillian. Two Regiments directors, Litha Nyhonyha and Magandheran Pillay, have subsequently gone to court to declare Wood a delinquent director. They are accusing him of sharing confidential company information with third parties, which, they say, paved the way for Trillian Capital Partners to make millions of rands in illicit payments from Transnet for work done by Regiments. The two directors claim that Wood had leaked company information to, among others, Salim Essa, in a bid to divert business from

Regiments to Trillian prior to the scheduled date of his departure and, in doing so, had caused the company severe reputational harm, court papers state.

Wood responded that he and the directors of Regiments had decided to break up the company but could not agree on how to apportion different parts of the business. In his view, the Transnet business belonged to him, so he took it with him. These claims became the subject of an independent investigation led by Advocate Geoffrey Budlender SC, appointed by then Trillian board chairperson Tokyo Sexwale.

In his report Budlender outlined the ways in which Trillian had obstructed the investigation and stated that for this reason 'the enquiry will not reach a satisfactory conclusion'. However, he also stated that 'these matters need to be fully investigated, the results need to be made public, and those responsible for any wrongdoing should be required to account'. Budlender went on to state that 'there is ample evidence in the public domain that malfeasance is continuing'.[61] The National Treasury is also investigating the Trillian–Transnet contracts.

Trillian had contracts not only with Transnet but also with Eskom, allegedly as a sub-contractor to McKinsey, dating back to September 2015. Although McKinsey has denied that it sub-contracted to Trillian as part of its Eskom work, we have seen a letter on a McKinsey letterhead dated 9 February 2016 and signed by McKinsey's Vikas Sagar, requesting Eskom to pay Trillian directly for services rendered. Furthermore, Trillian bank statements, seen by our researchers, show that it paid out R160 million to an unknown beneficiary (through the Bank of Baroda) on 14 April 2016 – the same day that Eskom paid Gupta-controlled Tegeta Exploration and Resources nearly R600 million to help buy the Optimum mine, a deal described in detail below.

In her *State of Capture* report, former Public Protector Thuli Madonsela presented evidence that Trillian and its subsidiaries had contributed R235 million of the R2.15 billion provided by a number of firms to enable Tegeta to pay for Optimum. Trillian has repeatedly denied this allegation without giving details. Indeed, the R160 million payment noted above seems more than a coincidence.

There is circumstantial evidence to suggest that the fallout between Regiments and Trillian was related to factional battles within the ANC over funding. Regiments had strong links to the Batho Trust, an investment vehicle established in the 1990s to support Thabo Mbeki's campaign. Batho later created the Thebe Investment Corporation, which became an important ANC fundraiser. We must ask whether the shift of contracts away from Regiments to Trillian was intended to sever this link with the ANC, and to redirect paybacks to a Zuma-aligned party-political faction. What is clear is that Trillian is involved in highly questionable dealings between SOEs and shadowy business groups.

The research project that produced the *Betrayal of the Promise* report observed how Trillian, for example, had written an advisory note for Eskom to grant the Duvha 3 power station contract worth R4 billion to Dongfang Electric Company, a Chinese SOE, even though, on technical specifications and price, Dongfang was initially disqualified by the procurement committee. The two companies that were front runners, General Electric and Murray and Roberts, suddenly found themselves out of the running. This is now the subject of a court battle, with General Electric challenging Eskom on the fairness of the tender award to Dongfang.[62]

The Guptas go transnational ...

In December 2014 it emerged that the Guptas were allegedly making use of the global financial system in what law enforcement circles refer to as 'shadow transnationalism' – an essential element for brokers facilitating large-scale criminality – to 'navigate resources to international clearing hubs, where they enter the legitimate trade and accrue value to the members of the network'.[63]

On 28 November 2014 Oakbay Resources and Energy listed on the Johannesburg Stock Exchange. Atul Gupta, his wife Chetali, brother Rajesh and sister-in-law Arti owned about 80 per cent of the company. Oakbay's main asset, and the main driver of its value, was its subsidiary, Shiva Uranium.

According to an amaBhungane investigation and documents seen by us, the Guptas, with the help of a Gupta associate in Singapore, appear to have inflated Oakbay's market value significantly above the inherent value given at the time. This allowed them to pay off a R100 million loan from the IDC, and also meant that the state-owned entity lost out when the Oakbay share price market-corrected.

At the time this story broke Oakbay's financials showed that it had not been able to maintain profitability at Shiva. According to the 2010 purchase agreement for the mine, the entire debt should have been repaid by April 2013. But Oakbay's financials stated that, by the end of February 2014, only R20 million had been paid and the debt, with interest, had grown to R399 million. In June 2014, after negotiations with the IDC, they agreed to restructure the debt, including a new repayment schedule that would end in 2018. As part of this agreement, and as Oakbay's pre-listing statement showed, the IDC would take a small stake (about 3.6 per cent) in Oakbay in lieu of the debt.

Oakbay's interim financials at the end of August 2014 gave the company a net asset value of about R4.6 billion, which translated into an asset value of R5.74 a share, according to amaBhungane.[64] This dropped to R4.84 a share once substituted with the lower value established by a valuer appointed as part of the listing requirements.

Despite this, Oakbay listed at R10 a share, which was nearly double the underlying asset value. This was significant because it was this R10 'market' value, minus a 10 per cent discount, at which the IDC received shares (its 3.6 per cent) in lieu of Oakbay's outstanding debt. Compared with the underlying value of R5.74 provided by Oakbay's own financials, or the adjusted R4.84, the IDC ultimately gave Oakbay a discount of between R93 million and R119 million (essentially cash in hand to clear its debt – an ultimate loss to South Africa given that these were state resources).

The question was how Oakbay had allegedly inflated its market value. The answer, according to an AmaBhungane investigation, lay in Singapore, where a company called Unlimited Electronic & Computers paid R10 a share in a private placement shortly before the listing, acquiring 2.3 per cent of the company. Unlimited Electronic & Computers, according to amaBhungane, is owned by Kamran 'Raj' Radiowala, who has been associated with the Guptas since about 2006.[65]

Online company registration data cited by amaBhungane reveal that Radiowala was appointed managing director of an Indian electronics distribution company, SES Technologies, in 2007. SES was co-owned by the Guptas' South African business, Sahara Computers, and its board included Ashu Chawla, one of the family's associates in South Africa. For some time the SES chief operating officer was George van der Merwe, who held the same position at Sahara and was the former CEO of Oakbay.

... and move their money offshore

In July 2015 amaBhungane presented the first detailed analysis of how the Guptas move the proceeds of their business activities. Their operation centres on a Gupta-controlled shell company called Homix. Shell companies, by virtue of the ownership anonymity they provide, are classic vehicles for money laundering and other illicit financial activity. According to the Financial Crimes Enforcement Network:

> The term 'shell company' generally refers to limited liability compa-
> nies and other business entities with no significant assets or ongo-
> ing business activities. Shell companies – formed for both legitimate
> and illicit purposes – typically have no physical presence other than
> a mailing address, employ no one, and produce little to no indepen-
> dent economic value.[66]

Between 2014 and 2015 Homix moved R166 million, primarily from 5 companies, through its accounts.[67] As is characteristic of shell companies, Homix has no discernible office infrastructure or staff commensurate with a company processing such large sums of money, according to amaBhungane, which visited its premises. Bank records obtained by amaBhungane, and other bank records seen by us, show that as money came into the Homix bank account it immediately went straight out again, to an equally obscure entity called Bapu Trading.

This pattern displays the three classic money-laundering characteristics of placement, layering and integration, where placement is the movement of cash from its source (the five companies), followed by placing it into circulation (layering) through, among other mechanisms, financial institutions and other businesses (for example, Homix), and finally integration, the purpose of which is to make it more difficult to detect and uncover by law enforcement.

Another example of the Guptas' attempts to externalise the proceeds of their operations (the placement phase) emerged six days after the Gupta family infamously 'fled' South Africa in April 2016 on a late-night flight. On 13 April 2016 a Gupta plane allegedly tried to leave with a box believed to have been full of diamonds.[68]

According to an amaBhungane investigation, a Gupta business jet was preparing to depart Fireblade Aviation's VVIP ('very, very important person') terminal at OR Tambo International Airport when X-ray scanners picked up something suspicious inside a suitcase belonging to the departing party.[69] In the suitcase was a box containing diamonds, amaBhungane claims (a claim that has not been refuted by the Gupta family). When Fireblade security staff asked to look in the box, a Gupta security staffer apparently refused, took the bag from the counter and left. Fireblade confirmed to amaBhungane that a 'potential security incident' had taken place early one morning in April 2016, but would not identify which client was involved.

The Guptas' immense offshore assets are noteworthy and, in money-laundering terms, may indicate the final stage of this process: layering (in which they 'legitimately' realise the value of their questionable gains). These are investments such as a Hindu temple they are building in India at a cost of R200 million and a villa in Dubai worth R448 million, which is listed as one of the most expensive houses in the United Arab Emirates. This does not include cash, which may be sitting in offshore accounts in, for example, Hong Kong, and which can be directed with ease as payoffs into their network.

Returning our focus to Homix, at some point the Reserve Bank became suspicious after payments from Homix to accounts in Hong Kong did not match claimed imports (misinvoicing is a classic money-laundering ploy) and froze some of the money. AmaBhungane investigations showed, however, how at least some of the money (R51 million not frozen by the Reserve Bank) that moved through Homix had been transferred out of the country into Hong Kong, where long-time Gupta associate Salim Essa is the family's placeholder in several shell companies (the leaking of the Panama Papers in 2016 showed that Hong Kong was the most active centre in the world for the creation of shell companies).[70]

The money went to two companies: YKA International Trading Company and Morningstar International Trade.[71] AmaBhungane could not trace YKA's sole director, a Chinese resident. Morningstar's registered director and owner is Mahashveran Govender, a South African, who is also untraceable. However, Morningstar's registered address in Hong Kong is the same as those of three other Essa companies, which are linked to the Guptas – Tequesta Group, Regiments Asia and VR Laser Asia.

Homix first emerged when amaBhungane broke the story of how national telecom company Neotel had benefited, with the assistance of Homix, from multi-million-rand Transnet tenders. Homix appeared to have positioned itself as a facilitator of state-owned company contracts. Despite Homix being virtually untraceable, Neotel's top managers had approved the payment to the Gupta company of tens of millions of rands in 'commissions' – ultimately more than R100 million – for no apparent work, according to amaBhungane, other than ensuring that Neotel got the Transnet deal.

In April 2015 Neotel's auditors, Deloitte, reported these unusual payments to Neotel's board of directors, questioning the 'commerciality' of the 'fees'. The money was billed as being in respect of contracts being secured with Transnet. Deloitte correspondence suggested that Neotel management had approved the Homix payments despite not knowing 'who this entity is'.[72]

The contract that appears to have precipitated the relationship between Homix and Neotel was a master service agreement to provide Transnet with a suite of telecom services worth hundreds of millions of rands a year. Neotel got the contract for an initial five years when it bought Transnet's in-house provider, Transtel, in 2008. At the end of 2013 Transnet put the master agreement out to tender. It was provisionally awarded to a competitor, T-Systems, but that company withdrew by agreement some months later when it became apparent that its solutions were inappropriate.

In April 2014, during this hiatus, Neotel paid its first R30 million to Homix, according to documents seen by amaBhungane and ourselves. The Deloitte correspondence identifies the payment as relating to routers and other equipment that Neotel sold to Transnet. Transnet is understood to have paid Neotel about R300 million for the equipment. Neotel's payment to Homix equals a 10 per cent 'commission'.

Four months later, in August 2014, Transnet notified Neotel that it was the new preferred bidder for the master agreement and that negotiations should be concluded before Christmas. But by early December individuals close to the negotiations were claiming that Transnet had become 'intransigent without clear reason'.[73] A week later, according to these individuals, Neotel's CEO, Sunil Joshi, met Transnet's chief financial officer, Anoj Singh, to whom the SOE's procurement structures reported. After the meeting Joshi allegedly asked his staff to approach Homix again.

A 'success fee' was agreed with Homix – 2 per cent of the R1.8 billion value of the master agreement with Transnet, equating to R36 million, plus R25 million in respect of a related agreement to sell assets to Transnet. Transnet then resumed negotiations and the master agreement was signed before Christmas.

Companies that paid money into Homix's bank account included Cutting Edge Commerce (R3.3 million between October 2014 and February 2015), of which the Guptas' Sahara Systems (a separate corporate structure from Sahara Computers) owns 51 per cent. Cutting Edge's website says it provides information technology and consulting services, and lists its public-sector clients as SAA, Airports Company South Africa and Transnet. Other companies involved were Regiments Capital (R84 million between November 2014 and March 2015) and Burlington Strategy Advisors (R1.8 million in March 2015).

Burlington Strategy Advisors, a subsidiary of Regiments Capital, signed a R5 million contract in March 2015 with German crane maker Liebherr Africa to provide it with market feasibility studies in relation to the supply of cranes to Transnet. Liebherr was a key supplier to Transnet, but the SOE was pressuring suppliers to include local companies in projects. In response, the German company signed the feasibility study agreement with Burlington and made an upfront payment of R2 million, according to amaBhungane. About 90 per cent of this was paid straight on to Homix, according to bank records subsequently obtained by amaBhungane.

It appears that the Guptas tried to obscure their link to Homix, but they failed. Company records list an unknown individual, Yakub Ahmed Suleman Bhikhu, as the company's only active director. But when Neotel's board commissioned a law firm in April 2014 to investigate the company's links to Homix, another individual, Ashok Narayan, emerged to answer questions, which served to confirm the Gupta link to Homix. Narayan was a former managing director of Sahara Systems. He was also a director of Linkway Trading, the Gupta company that had been a project consultant for the Free State Vrede dairy project in its early stages.

Enter Mosebenzi Zwane

On 22 September 2015 President Zuma – reportedly to the surprise of even top members of the ANC – announced that he would fill a six-month-old vacancy in his Cabinet with the relatively unknown Mosebenzi Zwane, whom he appointed to the critically important mineral resources portfolio. Zwane's appointment as a minister catapulted him from the parliamentary backbenches. Indeed, he had been plucked from the Free State provincial government, where, as Member of the Executive Council responsible for agriculture, he had facilitated the Gupta dairy farm deal. He had no experience in mining or in a national portfolio position. His origins in the Free State suggest that this was a move orchestrated by Ace Magashule.

In April 2016, seven months after Zwane's appointment, Gupta-owned Tegeta Exploration and Resources, an Oakbay subsidiary, acquired Optimum coal mine from Glencore, one of the world's largest commodity trading and mining companies, which is headed by a former South African. Duduzane Zuma owns 12.8 per cent of Tegeta. Various members of the Gupta family own 36 per cent of the company, Gupta associate Salim Essa owns 21.5 per cent, and just over 20 per cent is owned by two offshore companies registered in the United Arab Emirates, for which ownership details are unavailable.

Apart from the Koeberg nuclear power station outside Cape Town and the still modest renewable energy programme, most electricity in South Africa is generated from coal. One of the coal suppliers was Optimum mine, which was contracted to deliver 5.5 million tons of coal a year to the Hendrina power station at a price of R161 per ton (according to the report prepared by Dentons, an international law firm hired by the board in 2015 to conduct an investigation into major issues at the power utility).[74]

This was at the low end of what Eskom paid; most prices were in the range of R200–R400 per ton. There were also concerns about the quality of the coal coming from Optimum. The mine had shifted 30 kilometres from its original shaft and the quality was declining. When international coal prices began to decline the sustainability of the Optimum mine was called into question. Glencore's business model until then had been to use revenues from coal exports to subsidise the cost of local coal.

In 2013 Glencore invoked the 'hardship clause' in its contract with Eskom to trigger negotiations about a new contract. The company wanted an additional R115 per ton to make the Optimum mine viable. It was losing R100 million a month. Following lengthy negotiations, a proposal was submitted to the Eskom board on 15 April 2015. The decision was referred to CEO Brian Molefe, who refused to approve the proposed new terms. On 10 June he again refused any deal with Glencore and on 31 July 2015 the company went into business rescue.

Looking to sell the mine, Glencore met with the Guptas in Switzerland in September 2015, a meeting arranged and facilitated by Zwane, who has close ties to the Gupta brothers. The deal was finalised on 10 December 2015.

Reports suggest that Molefe had driven the mine into bankruptcy so that it could be bought by Oakbay. In addition, Tegeta did not actually have the R659 million needed to purchase the mine. On the evening of 11 April 2016 the Eskom board met and agreed to a R659 million prepayment to Tegeta for coal supplies. The

Oakbay company was essentially paid to provide a service from an asset it did not even own yet. The transaction was of dubious legality.

Business Day reported on 21 April 2017, claiming sight of a document from the Office of the Chief Procurement Officer, that the 'fiscus wants the prepayment to be declared irregular expenditure and Eskom to be investigated for failure to prevent irregular and fruitless expenditure'.[75] The document also suggested that Molefe be investigated for misleading the fiscus. At the time of the deal he had given written assurances that the coal in question met Eskom's requirements. It seems that it did not, and findings to this effect were suppressed by the Group Executive for Generation, Matshela Koko. What did happen was that the price of coal supplied by Tegeta rocketed from the R161 per ton paid to Glencore to R550 per ton (R700 per ton with transport). We see this in the massive expansion of contracts granted to Tegeta and other Oakbay mines, including Koornfontein, in 2016.

In her *State of Capture* report Madonsela found that Eskom may have repeatedly broken the law to accommodate Tegeta. This incident marks a key moment in the radicalisation of the Zuma administration and in the project of radical economic transformation.

Even before Tegeta bought Optimum, several red flags had been raised about the Gupta-owned company in its operation of the Brakfontein mine. In September 2015, a few months after Tegeta began supplying coal from Brakfontein, Eskom's coal scientist, Mark van der Riet, and a senior laboratory services manager, Charlotte Ramavhona, were suspended after conflicting laboratory results raised concerns about the quality of the coal Eskom was receiving from the mine. According to amaBhungane, the two were told they were being suspended following an alleged anonymous tip-off that Eskom had received about collusion in the laboratories.[76] Three independent sources alleged to amaBhungane that the suspension related to disputes over the quality of Brakfontein's coal and indeed, based on circumstantial evidence, this appears to have been the case.

A year later, in September 2016, a leaked draft report of a National Treasury investigation into the Brakfontein contract confirmed that the two had been correct to raise red flags. Despite Eskom's statements that the South African Bureau of Standards had approved the quality of Brakfontein's coal at the end of August 2016, subsequent tests found that the coal failed to meet acceptable standards.

In December 2015, while Van der Riet and Ramavhona were still on suspension and Tegeta's purchase of Optimum was being finalised, Tegeta was granted a short-term contract to supply 255 000 tons of coal a month to another power station, Arnot. It subsequently emerged that the award of this contract had resulted in Eskom extending Tegeta a R586 million (excl. VAT) upfront payment for this coal supply, six hours after the Gupta company's banks refused them a R600 million loan to close the Optimum coal deal.

The *State of Capture* report concluded that the payment was probably pushed through to plug a R600 million hole in the R2 billion the Guptas needed to buy Optimum. At a special late-night tender committee meeting on 11 April 2016 Eskom executives, led by Brian Molefe, agreed to transfer R586 million to Tegeta – money that was then used, two days later, to help pay for the purchase of Optimum.

About three months after the R586 million extension Optimum's business rescue practitioners, Piers Marsden and Peter van den Steen, filed a report with the Directorate of Priority Crime Investigation in terms of Section 34 of the Prevention and Combating of Corrupt Activities Act (No. 12 of 2004). Their concerns centred on the fact that while Eskom had claimed that the prepayment was needed to open new mining areas at Optimum's mine so that it could meet the requirements of delivering an additional 250 000 tons of coal to Arnot, the business rescue practitioners had not seen any of the prepayment, meaning that it had quite clearly been directed elsewhere and not into Optimum's accounts to assist with its liquidity, as stated by Eskom.

The draft findings of a year-long National Treasury investigation concluded in April 2017 that the prepayment should be treated as a loan. According to the report on the investigation:

> The advance payment of R659 558 079 should be regarded as a loan because there is no evidence that Optimum Coal Mine or Tegeta Exploration and Resources used the funds to procure any equipment for increasing the volume of the coal or further processing the coal.[77]

The investigators added that the interest should be recovered from Tegeta or from the Eskom officials involved. The draft report also recommended that a forensic audit firm be appointed to 'investigate why Eskom gave and continues to give preferential treatment to Tegeta ... by not enforcing key conditions of the Coal Supply Agreement'.[78]

In August 2016 Eskom acting CEO Matshela Koko gave Tegeta a R7 billion coal contract without a tender, ignoring warnings from the National Treasury that such a contract could be irregular.[79] Under the contract Tegeta's Koornfontein Mines would deliver 2.4 million tons of coal a year at R414 per ton to Komati power station. The contract was due to run until August 2023. However, two months after the seven-year contract was signed Eskom's board decided to mothball the power station. This means that Eskom will either need to buy Tegeta out of the contract or assume the cost of transporting the coal to another power station at least 50 kilometres away.

According to amaBhungane, the R7 billion contract is one of three lucrative coal contract extensions that Eskom tried to push to Tegeta over 15 days in August 2016. Treasury rejected two of the contracts (one a R855 million extension for the provision of coal to Arnot power station, without an open tender) but told Eskom it could sign the Koornfontein contract provided that strict conditions were met. Indications are that Eskom failed to meet the conditions, but signed anyway.

The Guptas move into the military

In February 2016 the Guptas emerged as beneficiaries in a deal with state-owned arms manufacturer Denel to profit from the sale of its products in Asia. This deal was another demonstration of how the family accesses and controls key board positions to gain personally from state resources.

In January 2016 Denel had announced the formation of a joint venture company called Denel Asia, but did not identify the Gupta family as shareholders. The announcement was made without approval from the finance and public enterprises ministers, as required under the Public Finance Management Act and in line with government guarantee conditions. Denel's lucrative Asian market – and, more specifically, a potential US$4 billion (R62 billion) tender to deliver long-range artillery to the Indian army – appears to have been the incentive for the deal.

In a press release announcing the joint venture Denel said that Denel Asia, headquartered in Hong Kong, would help Denel 'find new markets for our world-class products, especially in the fields of artillery, armoured vehicles, missiles and unmanned aerial vehicles'. Denel's joint venture partner in the company was identified as 'VR Laser, a company with 20 years extensive experience [in] defence and technology in South Africa'.[80] Denel also said that VR Laser had 'a good understanding' of the target 'markets and opportunities'. Hong Kong corporate records showed that VR Laser was founded on 29 January 2016 with Denel holding 51 per cent and Hong Kong shell company VR Laser Asia 49 per cent.

Interestingly, VR Laser Asia was registered in Hong Kong two years after the Gupta family and associates had acquired VR Laser Services.

Westdawn Investments, a Gupta contract mining company better known as JIC Mining Services, owns a 25 per cent stake in VR Laser Services and Salim Essa owns 75 per cent, according to shareholder records seen by amaBhungane. Duduzane Zuma acquired a stake through Westdawn. VR Laser's only two directors are Essa and Pushpaveni Govender; the latter is also a director of other Gupta companies. Kamal Singhala, a 25-year-old nephew of the Guptas, who gives his address as the family's Saxonwold compound, is a former director.

Momentum for the Denel/VR Laser joint venture appears to have built after Public Enterprises Minister Lynne Brown appointed a new Denel board in late July 2015. When Brown announced the new board she apparently abandoned a list of proposed directors prepared for her by the Department of Public Enterprises, which wanted to retain most of the existing board members on the basis that they had performed well and had not served their maximum two terms. The list Brown presented to Cabinet reportedly bore no resemblance to the one prepared by the department. Those on the list lacked skills and experience: there was, for example, not a single engineer (Denel being a highly technical company) and most had never served on a corporate board before. She retained only one member of the outgoing board, Johannes 'Sparks' Motseki, 'for purposes of continuity'.[81] Motseki, a former treasurer of the Umkhonto weSizwe Military Veterans Association, is a Gupta business partner. A company of which he is the sole director was allocated 1.3 per cent in the Gupta-led consortium that bought Shiva Uranium in 2010.

Once appointed, the new chairperson, Dan Mantsha, who was also the legal adviser to Minister of Communications and Zuma loyalist Faith Muthambi, suspended Denel CEO Riaz Saloojee, chief financial officer Fikile Mhlontlo and company secretary Elizabeth Africa. No formal reasons were given at the time, according to amaBhungane. He appointed Zwelakhe Ntshepe as acting CEO.

By March 2016 Denel was marketing its products at India's DefExpo under the banner of Denel Asia, although neither Brown nor then Finance Minister Gordhan had given the necessary authority for the formation of the joint venture (in fact, the National Treasury had described the formation of Denel Asia as illegal). At the time Minister Brown apparently held a report from law firm ENSafrica that raised red flags about VR Laser's proximity to so-called 'politically exposed persons' and concerns about the company's solvency. According to a source with insight into the transaction, Denel had offered its intellectual property to Denel Asia in return for a promise of a R100 million marketing contribution from VR Laser.

In May 2017 Finance Minister Malusi Gigaba ordered the dissolution and deregistration of Denel Asia.

Transnet continues to yield

In July 2016 it emerged that a Gupta-linked company was positioned to win the majority share of a Transnet contract worth R800 million, without a competitive tender.

Documents obtained by amaBhungane and the *Mail & Guardian* showed that in November 2015 the rail division of the parastatal had issued the tender for an information technology solution, but controversially 'confined' it to one bidder only, the business software giant SAP.[82] A condition of the tender was that 60 per cent of the value was to be spent on 'supplier development', a provision normally aimed at BEE.

This was well above the National Treasury's 25 per cent limit on sub-contracting and dwarfed Transnet's planned target of not less than 20 per cent. According to amaBhungane, when SAP submitted its bid in December 2015 it committed itself to placing the entire 60 per cent with one company, Global Softech Solutions. At that time Global Softech Solutions was half-owned by the Guptas' Sahara Systems, and the balance was owned by an associate of theirs.

In its bid documentation SAP told Transnet that the price it had quoted was pushed up by the 'risk' of sub-contracting such a large share of the contract to Global Softech Solutions, a company it had not used before. In response to questions from the media, Transnet said that 'suppliers appoint sub-contractors at their discretion'.[83] But in the bid documentation SAP suggested the choice lay with Transnet, stating: 'Should Transnet have a preference of an additional specific partner to engage with, SAP will be happy to review their skills and their resource matrix.' Oakbay Investments said in response to questions from amaBhungane that 'the notion that a global multi-national such as SAP, which has almost 300 000 customers in 190 countries and reports over €20-billion in annual revenues, could be pressured, is quite preposterous'.[84]

Transnet's technical team also appeared confused by the choice of Global Softech Solutions. Minutes of a January 2016 meeting between Transnet and SAP representatives to discuss SAP's bid note: 'SAP to use GSS [Global Softech Solutions] for local supplier development. Why only one entity? Where [is] GSS track record? Not provided.'[85] The minutes propose a meeting between Transnet's BEE manager, Abdool Lutchka, and 'Sunil' from SAP, understood to be Sunil Geness, SAP Africa's director of government relations, to discuss supplier development.

Global Softech Solutions is headed by Leela Yemineni, who, according to his LinkedIn profile, was educated in India and worked for Transnet as an SAP consultant for two years before starting the company in 2010. In July 2014 he was joined by an Indian citizen, Mukul Teckchandani. According to his LinkedIn profile, Teckchandani had been general manager of Sahara Systems since March 2014. On 8 September 2015, when the close corporation was converted to a company, Sahara Systems was allotted half the shares, with Yemineni retaining the other half. On 26 May 2016 Sahara Systems transferred its shares to a company called Futureteq. This was the same day Transnet's internal audit put a stop to the initial contract award process.

According to amaBhungane, Futureteq appears to operate from Gupta company premises in Midrand. Fehmeda Jeena, who owns 50 per cent of Futureteq, is the former head of new business development for Sahara Systems and Himanshu Tanwar, its digital transformation consultant, is a former marketing manager for Sahara Systems.

Treasury's bulwark: declaratory order

In the course of 2016, and providing the clearest signal that the Guptas were breaching financial regulations, South Africa's 'Big 4' banks – Standard, First National, ABSA and Nedbank – as well as auditor KPMG and advisor Sasfin ended their relationships with the family.

While they did not give detailed reasons for this, we have established that at least some of the banks based their decision on a serious financial regulatory breach associated with the family. On 14 October 2016 Minister of Finance Pravin Gordhan filed an affidavit showing how R6.8 billion in 'suspicious and unusual transactions' might have contributed to the decision by the banks to close accounts associated with the Gupta family.

The payments – made by the Gupta family and its companies in the preceding four years – were listed in a Financial Intelligence Centre report attached to court papers filed in the Gauteng division of the High Court in Pretoria. Gordhan, who was the sole applicant in the case, was asking the court for an order declaring that he could not interfere with the banks' decision to close the Gupta accounts. Gordhan had been under immense pressure to intervene, both from Gupta representatives and from within government. Correspondence attached to Gordhan's application showed that between April and September 2016 then Oakbay CEO Nazeem Howa had written repeatedly to Gordhan, trying to persuade him to influence the banks to reopen the accounts.

According to court documents, the Gupta companies and their executives claimed that they were the victims of an 'anti-competitive and politically-motivated campaign' and that the banks had provided 'no justification whatsoever' for closing their accounts.

At the end of July 2016 Gordhan wrote to both the Financial Intelligence Centre and the Registrar of Banks at the South African Reserve Bank asking if there was any evidence they could legally share that would indicate the banks were right to be concerned about the Guptas' financial dealings.

In response, Financial Intelligence Centre Director Murray Michell compiled a report listing financial transactions by Gupta family members and entities that banks had reported. The list included 52 transactions ranging from R5 000 to R1.37 billion, totalling R6.8 billion. It also included 20 multiple transactions for which no amounts were given. Michell wrote that the legislation did not permit him to give details of the banks' reports, but referred to the possibility of them being submitted to court.

Separately, Registrar of Banks Kuben Naidoo wrote to Gordhan that Standard Bank had informed the Reserve Bank's financial surveillance department about 'a particular foreign exchange transaction involving VR Laser Asia, an associated company of Oakbay, which could form the basis of an exchange control related investigation by that department'.[86]

The correspondence attached to Gordhan's affidavit also gives insight into a behind-the-scenes tug-of-war over the inter-ministerial committee that Cabinet had appointed in April 2016 to 'engage' with the banks on the Guptas' behalf. The committee was led by Mosebenzi Zwane, a Gupta loyalist. Gordhan, his affidavit shows, sought legal advice on whether there was any basis for him as minister of finance to intervene with the banks.

A resulting legal opinion, from advocates Jeremy Gauntlett and Frank Pelser, warned that not only was there no legal way he could intervene but that the planned meeting between ministers and the banks could have 'unintended consequences' and create 'adverse perceptions' about political interference in the banking sector. This was echoed in a letter to Gordhan from Lesetja Kganyago, the governor of the Reserve Bank, in which he wrote: 'We caution against the unintended consequences of this being viewed as undue political interference in banks' operations ... This could introduce heightened levels of uncertainty and pose a risk to South Africa's financial stability.'

In August 2017 the North Gauteng High Court dismissed Gordhan's application for a declaratory order that the finance minister could not get involved in a fight between the Guptas and the banks, saying that it was not necessary to make a declaratory order on a law that already exists.

In March 2017 the Bank of Baroda, which appeared to be one of the last financial institutions with exposure to the Guptas, announced that it was closing their accounts.[87] In response to the application brought by the family for an interdict to stop the bank from taking this action, in October 2017 the High Court ordered the bank to keep the accounts open pending a final application, which is still to be heard.

Buying a bank

With the Guptas' access to the domestic and global financial systems increasingly constrained, they engaged in what was perhaps a desperate and last-ditch attempt to externalise the proceeds of their deals: an ambitious bid to buy Habib Overseas Bank, through Gupta-linked Vardospan.

On the day, perhaps not coincidentally, that Minister of Finance Gordhan and his deputy, Mcebisi Jonas, were removed from their positions, Vardospan filed an urgent High Court application in Pretoria to compel regulators to rule on its application for a banking licence. Vardospan owners Hamza Farooqui and Salim Essa were seeking an explanation for why the Reserve Bank, the Registrar of Banks and the minister of finance had delayed their application for seven months. Ultimately the application was rejected after the courts ruled it was not an urgent matter.

The attempted purchase of the bank by the Guptas should be viewed as what it was: an attempt to circumvent and evade established financial regulatory requirements designed to protect South Africa from illicit financial behaviour. We have been told that Habib Bank became concerned about the identity and modus operandi of Vardospan after the buyer apparently offered to increase the purchase price by a considerable amount on condition that Habib helped to expedite the sale. Habib never accepted this.

The deals detailed in this chapter, which have greatly enriched the family and its collaborators, would not have been possible without the political leverage the family was able to deploy. To this extent their modus operandi fits the classic model of broker-cum-fixer rather than the image of all-powerful puppeteer. The aim of the deals has been to convert political leverage into commercial gain, while simultaneously guarding against over-dependence on a political marketplace the family cannot directly control.

To manage the risk involved, the Guptas either increase control where they can by ensuring others depend on them or diversify their portfolio beyond their narrow Zuma-centred network (which is, in turn, highly risky). The aim is to ensure that others become increasingly dependent on them, hence the establishment of transnational financial networks. As the Zuma-centred power elite came to depend more and more on a symbiotic relationship between the constitutional and shadow states, it became increasingly dependent on the Gupta networks for getting things done.

The information and reports cited in this chapter make it possible to identify a specific modus operandi that the Guptas have tended to follow when they set out to achieve an outcome. The first step is to create a legitimate commercial vehicle; this has usually involved Zuma family members as key beneficiaries. This enables two things: they can present themselves as BEE compliant, and they can bully those they deal with by claiming – often quite explicitly – that they have political endorsement at the highest level (that is, 'without us this deal won't go through').

Once they have established a negotiating position for themselves they have used their access to change the rules of the game. They have done this either through insider information about forthcoming policy or regulatory changes that they can either anticipate or manipulate to their own advantage, or by ensuring that the right decision-makers are in place in the right structure to make decisions that are favourable to them.

The use of Homix as a facilitator between Transnet and Neotel is a clear example of this – the most obvious question being why Transnet, with one of the biggest and most experienced treasury teams in the country, and Neotel, a national telecoms company with a R4 billion turnover, needed an obscure shell company to broker an information technology contract between them.

To achieve any of these ends the Guptas have been prepared to offer payments of various kinds – from straight bribes to rewards for services rendered and so-called 'commissions'. Having access to large amounts of money in cash makes this all viable. It also ensures future cooperation and pliability, since recipients become 'locked in' to their network as a result. Finally, they are masters at fronting, obfuscation, denial, intimidation and lying. That they have acted with such impunity points to their belief that they enjoy powerful political protection.

That they felt utterly untouchable was on display in 2011 when former Gupta spokesperson Gary Naidoo responded to a question about a questionable deal in the media sector.

It would seem that there are forces at play which are determined to find fault with the relationship between the president, the government and the Guptas. For the umpteenth time, let us repeat: a friendship has existed between the family and the president for many years and it goes back to way before the current president's ascent to power. For the record the family took a decision in 2007 to forgo all government tenders and contracts to stop the continuous insinuation of an improper relationship between government and the Guptas.

These attacks have intensified since the launch by the family of a national English daily newspaper and [the family's] entry into the highly contested mining sector. We remain surprised by some quarters of the media's continuous and malicious attacks on the president, the family and its business partners in the face of not a single shred of evidence. Rather, these attacks are based on conjecture and insinuation and innuendo. We are even more surprised by your focus on trying at all costs to find something improper in the family's entrepreneurship, rather than to recognise its innovation in creating jobs and growing foreign direct investment into South Africa. Finally, for the record, the family subscribes to the highest standards of governance and ethics (including proactive management of conflicts) in business and the continuous suggesting of impropriety is both tiresome and defamatory.[88]

Notes and references

1 Skiti, S. 2013. 'Guptas tried to buy SAA boss'. Available at: www.timeslive.co.za/sundaytimes/article790030.ece.

2 This chapter depicts the facets of Gupta-linked state capture as they have been reported in the South African media and elsewhere. The authors did not research the underlying facts, unless otherwise indicated, and the evidence is presented as a summary of published material and not as proof of the facts. Opinions expressed by the authors are based on the reports, assuming their veracity.

3 Sole, S & L Faull. 2013. 'R10-billion contract behind SAA dogfight'. Available at: http://amabhungane.co.za/article/2013-03-22-r10billion-contract-behind-saa-dogfight.

4 Zuma, J. 2016. 'If I were a dictator for just 6 months everything would be sorted'. Video. SouthAfricanism.com. The English translation of Zuma's words was given as subtitles on the video. Available at: https://www.youtube.com/watch?v=maINYSlsoq8.

5 Liebenberg, S. 2014. 'A proposed theory of war economies and a supporting policy framework for dismantling war economies in Sub-Saharan Africa'. Unpublished doctoral thesis, Nelson Mandela Metropolitan University.

6 Liebenberg. 2014. 'A proposed theory of war economies'.

7 Jagarnath, V. 2016. 'Ajay comes to Jo'burg: From selling shoes to assailing the state'. Available at: www.dailymaverick.co.za/opinionista/2016-10-28-ajay-comes-to-joburg-from-selling-shoes-to-assailing-the-state/#.WPsmqlN97UI.

8 Govender, P. 2011. 'From Saharanpur to Saxonwold: The incredible journey of the Gupta family'. Available at: www.timeslive.co.za/sundaytimes/stnews/2011/06/10/From-Saharanpur-to-Saxonwold-The-incredible-journey-of-the-Gupta-family1.

9   Govender. 2011. 'From Saharanpur to Saxonwold'.

10 Jagarnath. 2016. 'Ajay comes to Jo'burg'.

11 Jagarnath. 2016. 'Ajay comes to Jo'burg'.

12 Jagarnath. 2016. 'Ajay comes to Jo'burg'.

13 Jagarnath. 2016. 'Ajay comes to Jo'burg'.

14 Jagarnath. 2016. 'Ajay comes to Jo'burg'.

15 Myburgh, P L. 2017. *The Republic of Gupta: A Story of State Capture*. Johannesburg: Penguin Random House South Africa.

16 Myburgh. 2017. *The Republic of Gupta*.

17 Myburgh. 2017. *The Republic of Gupta*.

18 Charter, L. 2016. 'Gupta brothers are not my friends – Mbeki'. Available at: www.dispatchlive.co.za/news/2016/04/11/gupta-brothers-are-not-my-friends-mbeki/.

19 Myburgh. 2017. *The Republic of Gupta*.

20 Myburgh. 2017. *The Republic of Gupta*.

21 Govender. 2011. 'From Saharanpur to Saxonwold'.

22 Andrew, M & K Serino. 2010. 'Keeping it in the family'. Available at: https://mg.co.za/article/2010-03-19-keeping-it-in-the-family/.

23 Jagarnath. 2016. 'Ajay comes to Jo'burg'.

24 Sport24. 2010. 'CSA launch historic T20 match'. Available at: www.sport24.co.za/Cricket/Proteas/CSA-launch-historic-T20-match-20101102.

25 Financial Times. 2016. 'South Africa: The power of the family business'. Available at: www.ft.com/content/abd6e034-e519-11e5-a09b-1f8b0d268c39.

26 Brümmer, S. 2010. 'Zuma "meddled in mine buyout"'. Available at: http://amabhungane.co.za/article/2010-05-14-zuma-meddled-in-mine-buyout.

27 Brümmer. 2010. 'Zuma "meddled in mine buyout"'.

28 Ryan, B. 2010. 'Shield against the unknown'. Available at: www.fin24.com/Finance-Week/Cover-Story/Shield-against-the-unknown-20100528-2.

29 Brümmer. 2010. 'Zuma "meddled in mine buyout"'.

30 Brümmer. 2010. 'Zuma "meddled in mine buyout"'.

31 amaBhungane Centre for Investigative Journalism. 2011. 'Going off the rails'. Available at: http://amabhungane.co.za/article/2011-03-04-going-off-the-rails.

32 amaBhungane. 2011. 'Going off the rails'.

33 Creamer, T. 2011. 'Transnet, DPE deny outside influence on Molefe appointment'. Available at: www.engineeringnews.co.za/article/transnet-dpe-deny-outside-influence-on-molefe-appointment-2011-02-28/rep_id:4136.

34 Creamer. 2011. 'DPE deny outside influence'.

35 Sole & Faull. 2013. 'R10-billion contract'.

36 Sole & Faull. 2013. 'R10-billion contract'.

37 Sole & Faull. 2013. 'R10-billion contract'.

38 Sole & Faull. 2013. 'R10-billion contract'.

39 Sole & Faull. 2013. 'R10-billion contract'.

40 Brümmer, S & S Sole. 2016. 'Guptas' R51bn train grab'. Available at: http://amabhungane.co.za/article/2016-06-19-guptas-r51bn-train-grab.

41 amaBhungane team & M Letsoalo. 2014. 'Jacob Zuma links to "untouchable" SAA boss'. Available at: https://mg.co.za/article/2014-11-06-jacob-zuma-links-to-untouchable-saa-boss.

42 Brümmer & Sole. 2016. 'Guptas' R51bn train grab'.

43 Brümmer & Sole. 2016. 'Guptas' R51bn train grab'.

44 Brümmer & Sole. 2016. 'Guptas' R51bn train grab'.

45 Brümmer & Sole. 2016. 'Guptas' R51bn train grab'.

46 Brümmer & Sole. 2016. 'Guptas' R51bn train grab'.

47 Sole, S. 2014. 'Free State dairy project damned in treasury investigation'. Available at: amabhungane.co.za/article/2014-02-06-free-state-dairy-project-damned-in-treasury-investigation.

48 amaBhungane Centre for Investigative Journalism. 2013. '"Guptas" farm cash cows in Free State'. Available at: amabhungane.co.za/article/2013-05-31-guptas-farm-cash-cows-in-free-state.

49 Sole. 2014. 'Free State dairy project damned'.

50 Transnet. 2014. 'Transnet awards largest-ever locomotive supply contract in South Africa's history'. Available at: www.transnet.net/PressOffice/Press%20Office%20Release/Transnet%20awards%20largest-ever%20locomotive%20supply%20contract%20in%20South%20Africa's%20history.pdf.

51 Faull, L, B Bhardwaj, M Letsoalo, S Sole & S Brümmer. 2014. 'Transnet tender boss's R50-billion double game'. Available at: https://mg.co.za/article/2014-07-03-transnet-tender-bosss-r50-billion-double-game%20.

52 Faull, Bhardwaj, Letsoalo, Sole & Brümmer. 2014. 'Transnet tender boss's R50-billion double game'.

53 Faull, Bhardwaj, Letsoalo, Sole & Brümmer. 2014. 'Transnet tender boss's R50-billion double game'.

54 McKune, C, S Brümmer & S Sole. 2016. 'Transnet's shady Gupta loan deal'. Available at: http://amabhungane.co.za/article/2016-09-18-transnets-shady-gupta-loan-deal.

55 Sole, S, C McKune & S Brümmer. 2016. 'How to eat a parastatal like Transnet – chunk by R600m chunk'. Available at: http://amabhungane.co.za/article/2016-09-16-xhow-to-eat-a-parastatal-like-transnet-chunk-by-r600m-chunk.

56 Sole, McKune & Brümmer. 2016. 'How to eat a parastatal'.

57 Sole, McKune & Brümmer. 2016. 'How to eat a parastatal'.

58 Sole, McKune & Brümmer. 2016. 'How to eat a parastatal'.

59 Sole, McKune & Brümmer. 2016. 'How to eat a parastatal'.

60 Sole, McKune & Brümmer. 2016. 'How to eat a parastatal'.

61 Budlender, G. 2017. 'Report for Mr TMG Sexwale, Chairperson, Trillian Capital Partners (Pty) Ltd on allegations with regard to the Trillian group of companies, and related matters'. Instructed by S Sirkar, Herold Gie Attorneys, Cape Town.

62 Hofstatter, S & C Paton. 2017. 'GE claims Eskom favoured Chinese firm's bid, with backing of Trillian'. Available at: www.businesslive.co.za/bd/companies/energy/2017-04-26-ge-claims-eskom-favoured-trillion-bid/.

63 Liebenberg. 2014. 'A proposed theory of war economies'.

64 amaBhungane Centre for Investigative Journalism. 2014. 'Another state bonanza for the Guptas'. Available at: http://amabhungane.co.za/article/2014-12-04-another-state-bonanza-for-the-guptas.

65 amaBhungane. 2014. 'Another state bonanza for the Guptas'.

66 Department of the Treasury Financial Crimes Enforcement Network. 2006. 'The role of domestic shell companies in financial crime and money laundering: Limited liability companies': 4. Available at: www.fincen.gov/sites/default/files/shared/LLCAssessment_FINAL.pdf.

67 Brümmer, S, S Comrie, C McKune & S Sole. 2016. 'State capture – the Guptas and the R250 million "kickback laundry"'. Available at: http://amabhungane.co.za/article/2016-10-29-state-capture-the-guptas-and-the-r250-million-kickback-laundry-unpacked-in-full.

68 Comrie, S. 2017. 'Exposed: The Guptas and the "box of gems"'. Available at: http://amabhungane.co.za/article/2017-02-19-exposed-the-guptas-and-the-box-of-gems.

69 Comrie. 2017. 'Exposed: The Guptas and the "box of gems"'.

70 Price, M. 2017. 'Hong Kong takes aim at middlemen in wake of Panama Papers scandal'. Available at: www.reuters.com/article/us-hongkong-regulations-moneylaundering-idUSKBN15T33D?il=0.

71 Brümmer, Comrie, McKune & Sole. 2016. 'State capture – the Guptas and the R250 million "kickback laundry"'.

72 Brümmer, Comrie, McKune & Sole. 2016. 'State capture – the Guptas and the R250 million "kickback laundry"'.

73 Brümmer, Comrie, McKune & Sole. 2016. 'State capture – the Guptas and the R250 million "kickback laundry"'.

74 Dentons South Africa. 2015. 'Report in respect of the investigation into the status of the business and challenges experienced by ESKOM, instituted by the Board of Eskom Holdings (SOC) Ltd in terms of a resolution passed on 11 March 2015'. Cape Town: Dentons South Africa.

75 Phillip, X. 2017. 'Tegeta advance "must be converted to loan"'. Available at: www.businesslive.co.za/bd/companies/mining/2017-04-21-tegeta-advance-must-be-converted-to-loan/.

76 Comrie, S. 2016. 'Tegeta coal quality hopelessly non-compliant, says report'. Available at: http://amabhungane.co.za/article/2016-08-30-tegeta-coal-quality-hopelessly-noncompliant-says-report.

77 Comrie, S. 2017. 'R10bn in 15 days – another massive Eskom boost for the Guptas'. Available at: amabhungane.co.za/article/2017-04-22-r10bn-in-15-days-another-massive-eskom-boost-for-the-guptas.

78 Comrie. 2017. 'R10bn in 15 days'.

79 Comrie. 2017. 'R10bn in 15 days'.

80 Dludla, S. 2016. 'Denel expands its horizons'. Available at: www.iol.co.za/business-report/ companies/denel-expands-its-horizons-1977303.

81 Daily Maverick. 2016. 'amaBhungane: How Denel was highjacked'. Available at: www.dailymaverick.co.za/article/2016-05-29-amabhungane-how-denel-was-hijacked.

82 amaBhungane Centre for Investigative Journalism. 2016. 'Gupta-linked company set to score R800-million in Transnet IT solution tender deal'. Available at: amabhungane.co.za/ article/2016-07-24-00-gupta-linked-company-set-to-score-r800-million-in-transnet-it-solution-tender-deal.

83 amaBhungane. 2016. 'Gupta-linked company set to score R800-million'.

84 amaBhungane. 2016. 'Gupta-linked company set to score R800-million'.

85 amaBhungane. 2016. 'Gupta-linked company set to score R800-million'.

86 Comrie, S, S Sole & S Brümmer. 2016. 'Gordhan blows whistle on Guptas' R6,8bn "suspicious and unusual payments"'. Available at: www.dailymaverick.co.za/article/ 2016-10-15-amabhungane-gordhan-blows-whistle-on-guptas-r6.8bn-suspicious-and-unusual-payments/#.WSNELxQRqT8.

87 Mkokeli, S, R Bonorchis & A Antony. 2017. 'Bank of Baroda begins closing Gupta-linked accounts'. Available at: https://mg.co.za/article/2017-03-02-bank-of-baroda-begins-closing-gupta-linked-accounts.

88 Shamase, N, S Sole & S Brümmer. 2011. 'Guptas claim conspiracy'. Available at: https://mg.co.za/article/2011-02-24-guptas-claim-conspiracy.

4

Repurposing Governance

From conviction to ideology

The Polokwane revolt in the ANC was informed by a conviction that economic transformation as pursued after 1994 had produced an anomaly, if not a perversion: a small black elite beholden to white corporate elites, a vulnerable and over-indebted black middle class and a large African majority condemned to unemployment and dependent on welfare handouts to survive. The rise in the Gini coefficient between 1994 and 2009 lends credence to this view.

Most people in the ANC and the Tripartite Alliance believe that the RDP was jettisoned when the Gear strategy was adopted in 1996. 'Few,' noted Ben Turok in 2008, 'seem to have accepted arguments such as those advanced by Minister of Finance Trevor Manuel, immediately before the [Polokwane] Conference, that "Gear was the ANC government's macro-economic programme to implement the RDP"'.[1] Gear was widely slated as a self-imposed programme of structural adjustment. As a Cosatu briefing document from 2002 put it: 'The movement ... sharply warned against the danger of promoting the interests of a new elite over and above that of the majority who stood to benefit from national liberation.'[2]

The repudiation of the Thabo Mbeki administration at Polokwane was absolute. All six of the most senior ANC and government officials lost their positions. After Polokwane the earliest expressions of this conviction as a set of policy proposals came from the ANCYL. Articulating a vision of 'Economic freedom in our lifetime' – an adaptation of the famous ANC slogan from the 1940s, 'Freedom in our lifetime' – Julius Malema, then president of the Youth League, recalled the Freedom Charter's categorical imperative: 'The national wealth of our country, the heritage of South Africans, shall be restored to the people.' At the Youth League's National General Council in August 2010 he explained that '*Nationalisation of mines* is but one of the components of realising economic freedom in our lifetime, and we should never compromise on that principle'.[3]

Nationalisation was not the only alternative to the market-friendly approaches pursued after 1994. Cosatu, for example, was exploring how the economy could be reconstructed using an investment strategy that differentiated between six types of capital: publicly owned fiscal resources, publicly owned resources in the hands of parastatals, public-sector financial institutions, socially controlled resources, retirement funds and private capital.[4] The first two, and especially the second – capital held by parastatals – would come to form the main pillars of what would later be called radical economic transformation. The battle to transform the economy was shifting away from the economy itself to the state and, in particular, to who controlled government's procurement budgets.

Radical economic transformation and public procurement

The idea of using government's procurement budget to realise social and economic outcomes is not new.[5] It was the backbone of South Africa's racially exclusive 'developmental state' in the 1930s and formed a key platform of the apartheid project, especially in relation to cultivating a class of Afrikaner (nationalist) capitalists in contrast to English-speaking (imperialist) capitalists.[6] Today, moreover, the international development literature frequently extols the virtue of such a policy. From Turkey to Mexico, governments and development agencies seek ways to leverage their procurement spend to create or nurture local industries.[7] Travis Taylor and Murat Yülek, for example, argue: 'If developing country governments are shown to possess significant purchasing power in imperfectly competitive markets, a menu of traditional and non-traditional procurement contracts that can support economic development become viable.'[8]

Similar ideas had informed the redesign of South Africa's system of public procurement in the 1990s. The focus was on government's purchase of goods and services to incentivise the emergence of black-owned small- and medium-sized enterprises. It was a key idea in the New Growth Path and the economic vision issued by the Department of Economic Development and it gave meaning to the notion of South Africa as a developmental state.[9] These ideas were clearly in wide circulation at the time because Malusi Gigaba, after his appointment as minister of public enterprises in 2010, specifically mentioned them.

Table 4.1. Value of South African SOE procurement (2010/11)

	SOE	SOE procurement expenditure (R million)	Percentage of total government procurement expenditure
1	ACSA	2 200	0.26
2	City Power	1 500	0.18
3	CSIR	700	0.08
4	Denel	1 600	0.19
5	**Eskom**	**74 000**	**8.75**
6	IDC	226	0.03
7	PetroSA	12 000	1.42
8	SAA	14 800	1.74
9	SAPO	6 000	0.7
10	SARS	2 700	0.32
11	SITA	6 000	0.7
12	Telkom SA	13 000	1.5
13	**Transnet**	**70 000**	**8.3**
	TOTAL	**204 726**	**24.17**

Source: Based on DTI. 2011. 'Leveraging public procurement. Annual small business summit': 19.

In a document produced in 2011, however, the DTI complained that broad-based BEE (B-BBEE) considerations hardly figured in state procurement practices (see Table 4.1).[10] This was about to change.

In December 2011 the Cabinet approved the Preferential Procurement Regulations to align them with the B-BBEE Act (No. 53 of 2003). At stake, noted the DTI, was the possibility of using R846 billion in public investment programmes to transform the economy. During this time much of the thinking about preferential procurement was coming from the DTI. From 2009 it was a key member of the Advisory Council established in terms of the B-BBEE Act. It also acted as secretariat to this council.

In 2010/11 there was more than R200 billion in SOE spending to leverage in the interests of BEE. The lion's share was in only two companies, Eskom and Transnet.

Their R144 billion (17 per cent of the government's total procurement budget) constituted more than two-thirds of the total procurement expenditure in SOEs.

In 2014 Deputy Minister of Trade and Industry Mzwandile Masina announced that the department would seek to create 100 'black industrialists' in the next 3 years. The idea had first been mooted in 2012 by the Presidential Advisory Council on B-BBEE. Masina noted that this was part of government's 'radical economic transformation programme'.[11] This may have been the first time the expression was used in a government policy document.

> Over the next five years, a host of working opportunities will become available to South Africans. For example, a new generation of Black industrialists will be driving the re-industrialisation of our economy. Local procurement and increased domestic production will be at the heart of efforts to transform our economy, and will be buoyed by a government undertaking to buy 75% of goods and services from South African producers.[12]

In other words, radical economic transformation was an ambitious project, not simply to create black-owned small- and medium-sized enterprises but to control the commanding heights of the economy. Here was a vision of economic transformation that was not contingent on the reform of white business and did not depend on the goodwill of whites to invest in the economy, to employ black people and to treat them as equals. It is not difficult to see how and why this vision of radical economic transformation was and is compelling, even virtuous.

When he was still minister of public enterprises, Malusi Gigaba addressed the Black Management Forum. He told the audience: 'As government we are committed to the creation of a new generation of black industrialists who are "creators", "producers", "strategists" and "decision-makers".' He added, 'This is more than just an economic imperative but a *moral requirement*,' concluding that 'a strong black industrial class is a prerequisite for robust entrepreneurship and innovation in Africa at large.'[13]

If the vision was bold, its execution would have to be audacious. For radical economic transformation required the exercise of control over state procurement budgets; repurposing state institutions to focus on economic transformation, in addition to their official mandates; and displacing established white-managed and -owned companies from a variety of sectors.

The SOEs would be at the forefront of this initiative. Vast sums of money were concentrated in only 13 organisations, with the balance of R600 billion splintered across thousands of government procurement points.

Procurement reform (1994–2012)

Historically, South Africa, following what was then traditional international practice, operated a centralised procurement system. This was reflected nationally in the establishment of a State Tender Board. While each of the four provinces had its own tender board, these only enjoyed advisory powers. In addition, the larger municipalities made their own procurement arrangements, generally centred on their own tender boards. SOEs also had autonomous procurement powers.

The first major study of the politics of procurement in South Africa noted that the initial trigger for reform after 1994 was the desire to include emerging small and medium enterprises in government contracts. Traditionally these contracts had gone to established and big white-owned businesses.

> Procurement reform was therefore centrally predicated upon and explicitly justified as an attempt to merge the two sides of South Africa's 'dual economy', procurement being utilised as a lever to help include previously disadvantaged business-owners in the mainstream.[14]

In the 1980s concerns about the inefficiencies in developing-country procurement practices converged with the 'good governance' agenda, informed by the move to new public management discussed in the Introduction. In South Africa specifically, central tender boards were regarded as 'out-dated, cumbersome and unwieldy, both bad procurers and a bottleneck in the effective discharge of government responsibilities'.[15] This conclusion by the Procurement Forum – a body created to frame and generate consensus around the shape of impending reform, bringing together relevant departments and stakeholders – dovetailed with similar proposals and opinions emerging from both the Department of Public Service and Administration and the National Treasury. The result was the major decentralisation of the tender system.

The process of decentralisation only really started in 2003. Originally the Green Paper on Public Sector Procurement Reform envisaged a Procurement Compliance Office to oversee procurement centres in each department or agency. It would be the lynchpin of the new system, exercising high-level control over education and training and enjoying robust powers to monitor, audit, investigate and sanction. Yet the office was not established, falling victim to policy differences between the National Treasury and the Department of Public Works. Indeed, something resembling this office would only be created in 2012 – the Office of the Chief Procurement Officer – in the National Treasury.

For this reason there was a proliferation of procurement points across the state, with wide discretion to buy goods and services from the private sector in the absence of proper oversight. Whereas in the 1990s there were, perhaps, a dozen points of procurement, tens of thousands of procurement points emerged as decentralisation proceeded from 2000 onwards following the abolition of the State Tender Board.

The effects were quickly felt. The auditor general reported year-on-year increases in wasteful and irregular expenditure. Corruption levels rose. The system was out of control. From the perspective of the protagonists of radical economic transformation, the dissolution of the State Tender Board in 2000 must have been viewed as a shocking mistake. It eliminated a centre from which hundreds of billions of rands could have been controlled.

Whereas the move to new public management and the creation of the Senior Management Service Programme (discussed later in this chapter), in particular, provided a vehicle through which the public administration could be politicised, it also massively constrained opportunities to pursue economic nationalism.[16] It is hardly surprising, therefore, that one of the highlights of the ANC's 2014 election manifesto was the call for a State Tender Board. Explaining ANC policies at the time, President Zuma said:

> The state must buy at least 75% of its goods and services from South African producers. The state's buying power will support small enterprises, co-operatives and broad-based black economic empowerment.
>
> We will ensure that large public entities such as Eskom and Transnet buy specified goods for the infrastructure build programme locally ... to further prevent corruption, tender processes will be centralised under a central tender board.[17]

In effect, two competing models of 'bringing corruption under control' were emerging. The first was driven by the National Treasury, which sought to reinvigorate the idea of a Procurement Compliance Office by establishing the Office of the Chief Procurement Officer in 2013. Work done by the PARI in 2012 had shown that corruption was increasingly related to vulnerabilities in the procurement system.[18]

The Office of the Chief Procurement Officer was not intended to be a new state tender board but rather to oversee the system so that, in the words of its first officer, Kenneth Brown, 'the procurement of goods, services and construction works is conducted in a fair, equitable, transparent, competitive and cost effective manner in line with the Constitution and all relevant legislation'.[19] The office has focused on ensuring 'fair value' in contracts, open and effective competition, ethics and fair dealing, accountability and reporting and, lastly, equity. The last was the office's term for discussing preferential procurement. It is not difficult to see that the Office of the Chief Procurement Officer, like the Constitution, was based on the belief that BEE could be reconciled with fair value in tendering and competitive bidding.

The second model was driven by the power elite, with key actors like Brian Molefe and others, who were less confident that the fight against rent seeking could be reconciled with radical economic transformation by relying on the Office of the Chief Procurement Officer or the National Treasury. They viewed the problem as the procurement framework, more generally the Public Finance Management Act and, beyond that, the Constitution. Their solution was not to try to eliminate competitive corruption to access rents, but to repurpose state institutions to establish a centralised rent-seeking system that would cut out the lower-level rent seekers, who were prone to getting caught, making mistakes and, in the process, compromising wider networks.

Radical economic transformation and the shift to extra-legal means

It is common in today's South Africa, in public and academic discourse, to discuss the Zuma presidency and its associated networks simply in terms of corruption. Tom Lodge, Professor of Peace and Conflict Studies at the University of Limerick and well-known political sociologist, for example, suggests that increasingly within the ANC, leadership behaviour appears to be characterized by neo-patrimonial predispositions and, while formal distinctions between private and public concerns are widely recognized, officials nevertheless use their public powers for private purposes.[20]

In South African law the use of public office for private gain is the definition *par excellence* of corruption. Lodge mobilises several arguments to explain this turn of events.

The first is historical: 'From the 1950s the ANC was drawn into extra-legal and armed opposition, processes which led its leadership to incorporate criminal groups into its networks.'[21] The second is financial: 'The ANC believed it needed massive funding to win its first election and this set expectations for future contests in which it began to rely on resources generated by party-controlled enterprises or by politically motivated contracting.'[22] Thirdly, he proposes that as the ANCYL displaced the trade unions as the organised base of the party, so it 'became increasingly amenable to a politics in which authority is manifest in the exercise of personal power, conspicuous consumption, and individual generosity'.[23]

These are useful insights. They explain corruption as a consequence of the history of structural constraints on the ANC's finances and of its organisational culture. However, what we see from 2011 is a presidency and new appointees to state institutions increasingly prepared to play fast and loose with the law and the Constitution, not simply out of self-interest, but out of *political conviction*.

Let us return to the DTI document from 2011 discussed above. The department looked forward to a change in the Preferential Procurement Framework to bring it into line with the B-BBEE Act. At stake was the requirement to include empowerment criteria in the evaluation of tender bids, so that price was not the sole consideration. There were two imperatives at work, not necessarily in contradiction with each other, but theoretically distinct.

These were a *good governance* measure that required that procurement matters be considered against a standard of fiscal probity, efficiency and effectiveness, and a *political* criterion that sought to privilege the racial transformation of the economy.

We see precisely this tension expressed in Section 217 of the Constitution, which deals with procurement.[24]

(1) When an organ of state in the national, provincial or local sphere of government, or any other institution identified in national legislation, contracts for goods or services, it must do so in accordance with a system which is fair, equitable, transparent, competitive and cost-effective.

(2) Subsection (1) does not prevent the organs of state or institutions referred to in that subsection from implementing a procurement policy providing for–

  a. categories of preference in the allocation of contracts; and

  b. the protection or advancement of persons, or categories of persons, disadvantaged by unfair discrimination.

When these clauses are read together the full force of the dilemma becomes apparent. The Constitution assumes that there is no major tension or contradiction between, on the one hand, procuring goods and services in a way that is *fair, equitable, transparent, competitive and cost-effective* and, on the other, giving *preference* and *protection* to black South Africans. It is precisely this assumption that the protagonists of radical economic transformation have called into question.

While in theory these imperatives could be reconciled by finding suitably capable and cost-effective black-owned companies, in practice – and given the history of apartheid – they worked against each other. At least, that was the claim. As the head of the Black Management Forum, Dumisani Mpafa, complained in 2016, 'Any black entrepreneur would tell just how hard it is to penetrate the private sector because of long-established relationships, over and above the deliberate bias towards white-owned companies.'[25]

As long as price and experience were the overriding criteria for awarding tenders, the DTI, the Black Management Forum and others, including the Progressive Professionals Forum, which was central to the formulation of this model of accumulation, insisted that the 'rules of the game' were rigged against black businesses. At the National Broad-Based Black Economic Empowerment Summit in 2013, for example, delegates complained that the Public Procurement Policy Framework Act (No. 5 of 2000) was

> [a] major impediment in advancing the objective of B-BBEE in the public sector ... The PPPFA [Public Procurement Policy Framework Act] makes it impossible for black-owned companies to compete fairly with large companies. The Act puts in place a weighting of

80% on price and 20% on B-BBEE score for smaller tenders, and
90% weighting on price, with 10% weighting on B-BBEE for larger
tenders.[26]

Earlier in 2010 the Black Management Forum had proposed that considerations of race count for 50/100 points on the B-BBEE scorecard. Underpinning this narrative was a clear conviction that the economy was dominated by white business.

The project of radical economic transformation was cast in binary terms: black economic empowerment was being obstructed by the insidious forces of what came increasingly to be referred to as white monopoly capitalism. Chris Malikane, the Wits University-based economist who accompanied Malusi Gigaba into the finance ministry as an advisor, argued, for example, that after 1994 white monopoly capital had enjoyed 'unfettered dominance ... over all levers of power in all spheres of society'.[27] He suggested that this control extended both to the 'private sector' and to 'all apparatuses of the state such as government, the universities, the courts, the press, the security forces and political parties'.[28] What he calls credit-based BEE and affirmative action strengthened the hold of white monopoly capitalism by creating a black middle class and a black capitalist class beholden to it. However, Malikane also describes a second black capitalist class brought into existence through the state procurement system.

The battle that is now raging over the removal of the Finance Minister in particular, is led by white monopoly capital together with this credit-based black capitalist class, whose ownership and control of the state and the ruling party is being threatened by the rise of the tender-based black capitalist class, which also has links with the leadership of political parties by winning tenders with the State.[29]

Malikane portrays a tender-based capitalist class as locked in a life-and-death struggle with white monopoly capital (and its credit-based BEE allies) to overcome the colonial class structure. The protagonists of this position have increasingly depicted the existing legislative and institutional framework, including the National Treasury and the Reserve Bank, as fundamental obstacles. Malikane, therefore, calls for a broad front of workers and youths and progressive whites to support tender-based capitalists in smashing these institutions. The project of radical economic transformation has increasingly been set up against key state institutions and the constitutional framework on the basis of a critical reading of South Africa's political economy, and of the constraints the transition imposed on economic transformation. This was an analysis emerging from within the DTI and on the fringes of the ANC. It resonated closely with the readings of South Africa's post-colonial situation that insisted that 'white racism' was the principal obstacle to 'transformation' in the post-apartheid period, downplaying other considerations, including South Africa's peripheral location in the world economy, the financialisation of the economy or even the effects of government policy. However, it was not the historical position of the ANC itself.[30]

The National Treasury: empowerment and guarantees

There were two major reasons why the National Treasury posed a significant obstacle to the project of radical economic transformation. Firstly, its constitutional mandate placed it in a complicated predicament. In South Africa the terms of public procurement are not defined simply in statute (subject to legislative revision) but are inscribed in the ground law of the country. The National Treasury, itself a creature of the Constitution, had to try to reconcile BEE with considerations of fair value for the fiscus and for citizens.

When the protagonists of BEE thus insisted that 30 per cent of government contracts, especially in SOEs, be set aside for black-owned companies, irrespective of their experience, capacity or the price at which they offered to provide services or goods, the National Treasury baulked. Indeed, the more the institution insisted that government entities proceed in a way that was 'fair, equitable, transparent, competitive and cost-effective', the more controversial it became.

The second area in which the National Treasury caused ructions was its control of guarantees. In terms of the Constitution any withdrawal from the National Revenue Fund must be approved by Parliament. Hence a state subsidy would need parliamentary approval. This, in effect, is what the B-BBEE caucus was demanding – that a subsidy be given to black companies for doing business.

The bar for guarantees was, however, much lower. It only needed a letter from the minister of finance. With a guarantee, state entities could borrow from private lenders such as banks (though not from foreign governments) to finance their investment plans and pay the growing number of black-owned sub-contractors. This is, indeed, how SOEs in South Africa have tended to finance their investments. If government entities default on interest payments, banks have a 'first call' on the South African fiscus. In effect, guarantees shift the risk from the lending institution to the fiscus. It is thus not hard to understand why the banks liked them.

In principle, therefore, guarantees are issued on the basis that the borrowing institution has a sound business plan and a secure and adequate revenue stream, and is reliably managed. In other words, they are issued by the minister of finance on the basis that the loans will never be 'called in'.

Table 4.2, drawn from Chapter 7 of the National Treasury's 2017 *Budget Review*, shows the exposure of the fiscus to loans taken out by various state entities between 2014 and 2017.[31]

Table 4.2. South African government guarantee exposure (2014/15–2016/17)

R billion	2014/15		2015/16		2016/17	
	Guarantee	Exposure	Guarantee	Exposure	Guarantee	Exposure
Public institutions	**469.6**	**220.9**	**469.9**	**255.8**	**477.7**	**308.3**
Eskom	350.0	149.9	350.0	174.6	350.0	218.2
South African National Roads Agency	38.9	27.4	38.9	27.2	38.9	30.1
Trans-Caledon Tunnel Authority	25.6	20.8	25.8	21.2	25.7	20.7
South African Airways	14.4	8.4	14.4	14.4	19.1	17.9
Land and Agricultural Bank of South Africa	6.6	2.1	6.6	5.3	11.1	5.4
Development Bank of Southern Africa	12.9	4.1	13.9	4.4	12.7	4.2
South African Post Office	1.9	0.3	4.4	1.3	4.4	3.9
Transnet	3.5	3.8	3.5	3.8	3.5	3.8
Denel	1.9	1.9	1.9	1.9	1.9	1.9
South African Express	1.1	0.5	1.1	0.5	1.1	1.0
Industrial Development Corporation	1.6	0.3	2.0	0.2	1.9	0.2
South African Reserve Bank	7.0	–	3.0	–	3.0	–
Independent Power Producers	**200.2**	**96.2**	**200.2**	**114.0**	**200.2**	**125.8**
Public–private partnerships	**10.1**	**10.1**	**10.3**	**10.3**	**10.9**	**10.9**

Source: National Treasury. 2017: 92

Eskom, with its R218 billion in 2016/2017, has by far the largest exposure to the banks. SAA's exposure increased to R17.9 billion in 2016/2017 from less than half that in 2014/2015.

Generally, South African ministers of finance have been careful about issuing guarantees, balancing the country's exposure with an assessment of the borrowing organisation's financial viability, for should this deteriorate, the risk increases that the fiscus will be required to purchase the original debt. The National Treasury has, therefore, been loath to extend further guarantees to SAA. The company is effectively bankrupt. So, too, is the SABC.

It is not hard to see why the National Treasury has, until now, been preoccupied with how state entities, especially Eskom, are governed, and beyond that, with the sovereign reputation of the state. If Eskom's debts became repayable it would have bankrupted the economy. South Africa came close to this position towards the end of 2016 when the World Bank threatened to call in its loans to Eskom. This threat arose from a complaint lodged by the Spanish government with the World Bank that Eskom was reneging on its commitment to sign the independent power producer contracts. The Spanish government laid this complaint because a number of Spanish companies have contracts in South Africa to build and operate renewable energy power plants.

The crisis was averted when the deputy minister of finance intervened, undertaking to convince the minister of energy to get Eskom to sign the contracts. In April 2017 both the deputy minister of finance and the minister of energy lost their jobs, and these contracts were never signed.

Also related to energy procurement, Nhlanhla Nene, and later Pravin Gordhan, became major obstacles to the nuclear build programme involving Russia when they made it clear that they would not approve the requisite loan guarantees.[32] Both subsequently lost their jobs.

There is an important subtlety to note here. Radical economic transformation via the SOEs is not devoted to any *particular* investment project, but is focused on continuing investment. In this regard, the nuclear deal is not so much about nuclear energy as it is an excuse for massive industrial expenditure. This is a clear example of repurposing an institution or a project for a goal that, at best, may or may not align with government policy and, at worst, may fly in its face.

No referenced research has contradicted the findings of the CSIR, which argues overwhelmingly in favour of renewable energy for South Africa as the cheapest and safest route to meeting the country's baseload needs.[33] In other words, nuclear power is undesirable because it is both unaffordable in current circumstances and is the wrong energy solution, without even taking into account its safety risks.

Radical economic transformation in practice

As the concept of radical economic transformation gained momentum within sections of Jacob Zuma's power elite, the National Treasury increasingly became the object of frustration. The trigger for this may have been the perceived insincerity of the minister of finance in respect of changes to the Treasury's regulations on preferential procurement.

There were steps taken in 2009 to align this framework with the codes of B-BBEE and particularly to bring the SOEs under the auspices of the B-BBEE codes. In 2009 Treasury announced that, with the DTI, it had revised its preferential procurement regulations to align with the B-BBEE Act.[34] On 6 June 2011 Minister Pravin Gordhan promulgated corresponding National Treasury regulations. On the same day he extended the remit of these regulations to include SOEs.[35] Yet six months later, almost to the day, he reversed his decision: 'I, Pravin Gordhan exempt the institutions [listed in Schedules 2, 3B and 3D of the Public Finance Management Act] from the provision of the Preferential Procurement Regulations.'[36]

The schedules in question listed all major public entities, including the very companies that the DTI saw as the advance guard of economic transformation, as well as government business enterprises. In other words, Gordhan had excluded the SOEs from the remit of B-BBEE. It must have seemed a clear signal to the Zuma-centred power elite and the protagonists of radical economic transformation that the National Treasury was not prepared to play ball.

There had been regular and major changes to the Zuma Cabinet – almost as though the president was experimenting with different configurations of people, alliances and departments. Between October 2010 and March 2017 there were 15 Cabinet changes, with rapid turnover in the 3 years between 2012 and 2014.

Of special strategic importance were the appointments to the Ministry of Public Enterprises, which acts as the majority shareholder in the two most important SOEs, Transnet and Eskom. On 31 October 2010 Barbara Hogan was removed as minister of public enterprises and replaced by Malusi Gigaba, who was an early, vocal supporter of using the procurement budgets of SOEs to pursue economic transformation.[37]

Transnet and Eskom

From the start of Brian Molefe's tenure as Transnet CEO there was a move to commission large-scale industrial projects, procure key services and goods from private companies and displace established, ostensibly 'white' firms from government work in favour of selected beneficiaries. Together with Transnet's chief financial officer, Anoj Singh, Molefe announced bold plans to procure new locomotives for the transport of coal and iron ore to Richards Bay. The project was worth R51 billion. The tender was published in October 2013 and the process was to be overseen by Iqbal Sharma, chairperson of the Board Tender Committee.

A key aspect of the tender was that it required that 60 per cent of the locomotive components be sourced locally. It was a major opportunity for local manufacturing companies. VR Laser, a company that already had a long-established relationship with Denel, was a strong contender. As detailed in Chapter 3, Sharma had an interest in VR Laser.

What is important about this case is that it set the pattern for other and larger deals. Four steps have become a kind of 'repurposing modus operandi'. They are that a new minister changes the board composition of an SOE, in this case Transnet; the SOE announces a major new acquisition or build project; people brought onto the board are either strongly in favour of radical economic transformation or have close personal links to some of the bidders (or both); and the tender is awarded in circumstances in which there is a clear conflict of interest.

One of the most flagrant examples of this manipulation of the procurement process happened at Eskom. In December 2014 there was another Cabinet reshuffle. This time Gigaba was moved to the Department of Home Affairs and Lynne Brown was installed as minister of public enterprises. Brown changed the Eskom board and brought Molefe over from Transnet as the CEO.

The public protector noted that almost all the new appointees to the Eskom board had links to the Gupta family.[38] Nazia Carrim was the wife of Muhammed

Sikander Noor Hussain, a family member of Salim Essa. Romeo Khumalo was a director alongside Essa at Ujiri Technologies. Mark Pamensky was a former director of the Guptas' Oakbay Resources and Exploration. Kuben Moodley was a special advisor to the minister of environmental affairs. Mosebenzi Zwane was a director of one of Pamensky's companies. Marriam Cassim had once worked at Sahara Systems – owned by the Guptas. Ben Ngubane was also a director, with Salim Essa, of Gade Oil and Gas. As the board chairperson of the SABC he had overseen controversial deals between the broadcaster and ANN7, the Guptas' television station. Devapushum Viroshini Naidoo was also Kuben Moodley's partner.

Those board members who were not part of the right network were quickly removed.[39] The Eskom board, in other words, was a tangled web of mostly undeclared personal and business associates, all linked to Salim Essa and the Gupta family. This was the context within which Eskom began to renegotiate some of its coal supply contracts, as detailed in Chapter 3.

During this period, the public protector found, Molefe called Ajay Gupta no fewer than 44 times and Ajay Gupta called Molefe a total of 14 times. Even more dramatically, in the run-up to the signing of the Tegeta deal, between August and November 2015, Molefe could be placed in the Saxonwold area on 19 occasions.[40] Given the obvious conflicts of interest and the fact that Jacob Zuma's son, Duduzane, had a major stake in the company (through his 45 per cent share of Mabengela Investments, which, in turn, owned 28.5 per cent of Tegeta), the whole deal was probably unlawful.

The price of coal supplied by Tegeta rocketed from the R161 per ton paid to Glencore to R550 per ton (R700 per ton with transport). We see this reflected in the massive expansion of contracts granted to Tegeta and other Oakbay mines, including Koornfontein, in 2016. The website of the Office of the Chief Procurement Officer, which provides information about contract deviations and expansions, currently only has information for 2016. In the second quarter of the year it recorded that a Tegeta contract to supply Eskom's Majuba power station was increased from R3 794 748 750 by an additional R2.9 million. Another Tegeta contract, to supply coal to the Arnot power station, rose by R854 955 000 from the original value of R235 021 150. The contract of the Koornfontein mine, owned by Tegeta, for the provision of the Komati power station, was increased by a further R341 544 200. In the third quarter of 2016 the original figure was increased by a further R6 955 200 000 – a 2 000 per cent escalation.

In effect, as the Dentons report (cited in Chapter 3) makes clear, Eskom was paying massive rents to third parties for the same coal it had previously bought cheaply. Undoubtedly, some of this money was for self-enrichment. Research by the PARI, however, suggests that it is possible that some of it went into the coffers of the ANC or, more precisely, the Zuma faction, to fund its internal campaigns and struggles.[41]

What happened at Eskom was nothing short of audacious. The SOE had leveraged its procurement budget to displace an established corporation in favour of a newcomer with strong links to the proponents of radical economic transformation. As much as this smacked of corruption, from the perspective of these proponents the Guptas were a useful 'battering ram' to displace white monopoly capital. The trouble was that Glencore, the displaced corporation, was a largely black-owned and -controlled firm.

The National Treasury's insistence that SOEs conduct themselves lawfully and award procurement contracts based on fairness, equity, transparency, competitiveness and cost-effectiveness made it a permanent thorn in the side of the Zuma administration. The first moves against it started in December 2015 when then Minister of Finance Nhlanhla Nene was unceremoniously dismissed and replaced by an unknown party backbencher, Des van Rooyen, who had links to the Gupta family. After a tumultuous weekend, during which confidence in both the government and the value of the rand plummeted, Van Rooyen was removed and replaced by Pravin Gordhan, Nene's predecessor.

Gordhan's return represented a temporary setback for the proponents of radical economic transformation. On 30 March 2017 he was fired again, and replaced by someone sympathetic to the project – Malusi Gigaba, the very person who, as minister of public enterprises, had restructured a number of SOE boards to manage the type of rent-seeking practices described above.

Fragmenting the political centre

As long as the project of radical economic transformation was pursued within the framework of the Constitution and the law, it was possible to use the architecture of government and the institutions of the state to discipline its great variety of actors and coordinate its multiple moving parts: boards of SOEs, their CEOs and their officials and staff at many levels, ministries and departments and the ANC.

But historically, and into the transition, this is a role that the ANC has wanted for itself. In numerous organisational reports and various strategic documents the ANC insists that it is a movement, rather than simply a political party, precisely because of its special duty to 'lead society'. This goes a long way towards explaining the dramatic politicisation of the public service in South Africa after 1998.[42] Originally intended to have a maximum of 3 000 members at senior management level, by 2005 it comprised 7 283 people, most of them in national departments. By expanding the size of the programme, the ANC tried to establish political control of the state. The organisational renewal document produced by the movement in 2017 identified limited political control of the state as its major problem: the ANC's influence was waning.[43]

The document cited three strategic decisions as the causes of this: the shrinking of the influence of Luthuli House, the ANC's head office in Johannesburg, and the ceding of certain responsibilities to government; the establishment of coordination structures at various levels; and the setting up of 'governance committees' in all legislatures.

In this context, the ANC complained of 'insidious internal strife' and 'factional battles for power', the loss of 'organisational capabilities', growing distance from the 'masses' and the tendency of the organisation to focus on fundraising instead of implementing its policies.[44]

As the ANC weakened and fragmented, the prospect of managing radical economic transformation through the movement became a chimera. Indeed, the organisation's electoral fortunes declined precipitously during Jacob Zuma's presidency and it is experiencing a major revolt from within, especially from members committed to democracy and the constitutional framework.

These divisions have also weakened the Cabinet as a stable centre of political control. The clearest and most disturbing indication that the South African rent-seeking system tends towards chaos is the collapse of the Cabinet system as the core of the executive branch of the state. Cabinet meetings under Zuma were badly managed, poorly chaired and informalised. Partly as a result of this, Cabinet decisions were no longer regarded by independent-minded, professional, uncorrupted senior departmental officials as strategically significant. Decisions were only regarded as significant if they had been endorsed by a specific network with reference to the wishes of President Zuma.

When Zuma was asked by a network to consider an initiative he invariably supported it, thus diluting the value of his strategic judgement. It was also well known that the suggestion from the last person to brief the president was the one the president would support. Hence the competition to gain access to him just before Cabinet meetings or key public appearances.

Everyone knew that it was easy to say they had Zuma's support. What really matters is not so much what he personally supported or what Cabinet had resolved, but what a particular network wanted to see happen. In other words, Zuma did not support initiatives as such; he anointed particular networks that could then activate initiatives in his name in return for rents. Zuma's role included activating actions to penalise those who did not conform (including the use of bogus intelligence reports, cutting off access to rents, removal and sidelining). Cabinet approval was secured only when needed, and not because there was a wider strategic plan that it saw itself implementing.

Cabinet, moreover, was no longer supported by a strong professional policy support unit like the Policy Coordination and Advisory Service headed by Joel Netshitenzhe in the Mbeki era. That unit filtered what went through to Cabinet, and managed the integration process as best it could. Although the Department of Planning, Monitoring and Evaluation (as it was called after the 2014 NMOS) came closest to playing this role, its mandate was too broad and unwieldy and it was never allowed to play the same role with regard to Cabinet.

When issues that came to Cabinet did need further attention and resolution, Zuma's preference was to establish ad hoc inter-ministerial committees, invariably populated by a group of loyalists and members of the state security establishment. These committees effectively ratified the wishes of the Zuma-anointed networks, thus endowing them with a veneer of Cabinet or executive authorisation. When a committee brought a matter for decision to Cabinet it was invariably rubberstamped and hardly ever debated.

On numerous occasions Cabinet ministers confronted an issue for the first time only when it was brought to them for a decision. In these cases, supporting documentation had not been circulated beforehand and key agencies such as the National Treasury, the Department of Planning, Monitoring and Evaluation or even a professional specialist unit in the relevant department had not been given a chance to inform the decision that Cabinet members were obliged to make. There was a general assumption that if the issue had come via a member of a particular 'in-group' and Zuma supported it in ways that the in-group seemed to understand, the role of Cabinet was to endorse whatever decision had been made elsewhere.

Cabinet approval of the nuclear deal was a case in point. At no time during the process had a plan been presented to Cabinet. The only documentation shown to them was the presentation on nuclear costing made by former Finance Minister Nene, a few hours before he was called by Zuma to a meeting and fired.

Political power had fragmented across the state and society, condensing momentarily in fleeting and fluctuating networks, few with formal power, most operating in the shadows and all heavily contested. In this context of unstable political relations, the Gupta–Zuma nexus came to be a relatively constant site of authority. It was an attractive one, moreover, because it could marshal substantial resources and was armed with the capacity to undertake propaganda. In other words, the Guptas served as 'fixers' in a project that was always at risk of spinning out of control.

Saxonwold, however, hosted only one of what we have called 'kitchen cabinets', through which contemporary political power in South Africa is exercised. There are others, including the 'Premier League' of provincial barons and networks in parts of the state and police intelligence agencies.

Ballooning of the Senior Management Service Programme

The fragmentation of power across the state and its retreat into shadowy networks outside the formal architecture of government has been compounded by the ballooning of the public service in the Zuma period. Vinothan Naidoo has conducted a methodologically innovative study of what he calls the 'machinery of government'.[45] Tracking the number of national government departments and entities from 1994 he finds, unsurprisingly, that there was growth and also fluctuation in the number of departments and entities in the Mandela period, as the new administration experimented with different configurations. In 1999 the number of departments and entities peaked at 30, and then settled at just below that number.

There was stability in this number of departments and entities during the Mbeki era. Then the number of public entities proliferated to more than 250 in 2008. This proliferation coincided with the influence of the new public management thinking on the organisation of the state, and the move to introduce 'business principles' into the structuring of government to improve efficiency.

In 2009, two years after the Polokwane conference and the year in which Jacob Zuma was sworn in as president, the number of government departments and entities spiked sharply. New departments were established and several were split in two. The Department of Provincial and Local Government was divided into the Department of Cooperative Government and the Department of Traditional Affairs. Likewise, two separate administrations were hived off from the Department of Education – the Department of Basic Education and the Department of Higher Education and Training. The same happened to the Department of Environment and Tourism.

Sometimes departments were renamed, and sometimes entirely new institutions were created – the Department of Planning, Monitoring and Evaluation, the Department of Women and the Department of Economic Development. All in all, there were 15 'big bang organisational events' with Zuma's coming to power, compared to 14 in the entire prior period since 1994, and with them, an escalation in the number of ministers, deputy ministers and directors general and a proliferation of government administrations. 'The rationale for expanding the number of national departments was officially based on a strategic assessment of policy and functional demands,' notes Naidoo. He adds that 'there is ... reason to doubt the integrity of this view, based on heightened patronage pressures exerted on President Zuma following an acrimonious succession from Mbeki, coupled with questionable rationale behind the creation of some departments'.[46]

In other words, it is far from clear that the ballooning of departments was motivated by the desire to improve the effectiveness of government. Such a large growth in the government system, with a huge expansion in the Cabinet, compounded already severe problems of coordination. It was accompanied, not surprisingly, by the growth of the shadow state and the move to find more manageable centres of control and management outside the state in more personalised networks – 'kitchen cabinets'.

What is more, the organisation of the state came to be based less on functional criteria than on political ones, and was accompanied by the politicisation of state administrations. Of central importance in this regard has been the Senior Management Service Programme. Established in 2001 to transform the civil service from a bureaucracy into a service organised on the model of new public management, it quickly became the preferred way of bringing the public service under political control. As discussed above, by 2005 it had grown from an intended 3 000 employees to more than 7 000, and may have swelled to more than 10 000 people today.[47] Work done by the PARI indicates that turbulence and dysfunctionality in government administration are often related to competition among different ANC, government and constitutional bodies competing for the right to appoint officials to key state positions.[48] In other words, the ballooning and politicisation of the state has come at the expense of functionality.

Investigations and prosecutions

As the Zuma administration radicalised, it became dependent on managing increasingly complex relations, many of them involving people engaged in unlawful activities. Zuma moved to establish control over key state institutions, especially those involved in criminal investigations and prosecution: SARS, the Directorate of Priority Crime Investigation (the 'Hawks') and the NPA.

In September 2014 Zuma appointed Tom Moyane as the new commissioner of SARS, summarily informing Finance Minister Nene of the appointment. SARS had been one of the major achievements of the ANC government, developing into a highly efficient revenue service, dramatically increasing tax compliance after 1998 and frequently delivering 'windfall' taxes to finance the growing welfare state. It had worked to simplify tax-paying procedures and improve customer service, while simultaneously building its capacity to detect and pursue delinquent taxpayers.[49] By 2014 the agency was beginning to run up against politically connected people involved in a variety of illicit activities, some of them associates of the president and his family, as well as businessmen known to be financial contributors to the ANC.[50]

A dossier appeared in October 2014 alleging that senior investigators at SARS, located in the Special Projects Unit, constituted a 'rogue unit'. Among other things, it was said that they were illegally spying on the president. Poor journalistic standards at the *Sunday Times* saw these allegations appear in more than 30 articles between August 2014 and April 2016. The *Sunday Times* has since issued an apology.[51] It was also found guilty by the press ombudsman of 'inaccurate, misleading and unfair' reporting.[52]

The reports were, nonetheless, used by the new SARS commissioner to launch an investigation into 'rogue' activities at SARS and to suspend the former (acting) commissioner, Ivan Pillay, as well as most of the agency's investigative staff, led by Johann van Loggerenberg. As a result, numerous high-profile and politically sensitive cases have simply stagnated or never been closed.

Securing a loyal intelligence and security apparatus

Between December 2009 and the end of 2017 there was a series of upheavals in the NPA, the Crime Intelligence Unit (a unit within the South African Police Service) and the Hawks.

The NPA

In December 2009 Zuma appointed Menzi Simelane as director of the NPA, an appointment held by the Supreme Court of Appeal in December 2011 to have been invalid. Simelane was suspended.

In December 2010 Nomgcobo Jiba, reportedly close to Zuma, was promoted to deputy director of the NPA. When Mxolisi Nxasana was appointed NPA head in October 2013 he clashed with Jiba and laid criminal charges of perjury against her (see below). In September 2016 Jiba was struck off the roll of South African advocates and placed on special leave.

In July 2014 Zuma began a process to remove Nxasana from his position and in May 2015 'agreed' to let Nxasana resign. He was paid R17 million, the balance of his 10-year contract.

Nxasana filed an affidavit in a case brought by civil society organisations relating to the review of the payout. In his affidavit Nxasana directly contradicts the affidavit filed by President Zuma stating that Nxasana wanted to leave of his own volition. Nxasana said under oath that 'it was never my intention to make a request to leave the office, nor did I ever make such a request to the President' and 'the president's version in this regard is false'.[53] In December 2017 a full bench of the High Court ruled that the contract termination was invalid and that Nxasana must pay back the R17 million.

In June 2015 Zuma appointed Advocate Shaun Abrahams as NPA head. In the same judgment as the Nxasana decision, the High Court ruled that Abrahams's appointment was invalid and it was set aside.

The Hawks

In June 2012 Nomgcobo Jiba suspended and instituted charges against Major General Johan Booysen, former head of the Hawks, who was investigating corruption charges against reported presidential ally Thoshan Panday. Booysen was accused of running a 'hit squad' in Cato Manor in KwaZulu-Natal – charges that have routinely been thrown out of court. The charge of perjury against Jiba referred to above related to statements she had made under oath in connection with the Booysen matter.

In May 2014 Zuma appointed Nathi Nhleko as minister of police. In December 2014 Nhleko suspended Hawks head Anwar Dramat on the grounds that he was implicated in the illegal rendition of Zimbabweans to their country of origin. Dramat was reportedly about to launch an investigation into the R246 million of public money spent on upgrading President Zuma's home in Nkandla. In the same month Nhleko appointed Lieutenant General Mthandazo Berning Ntlemeza as acting head of the Hawks. In January 2015 Ntlemeza suspended Major General Shadrack Sibiya, former head of the Hawks in Gauteng, on the same grounds as those used to justify the suspension of Dramat.

When the Independent Police Investigative Directorate, headed by Robert McBride, cleared Dramat of wrongdoing, McBride himself was illegally suspended by Nhleko in March 2015. The decision was later overturned in a landmark judgment by the Constitutional Court, which confirmed the independence of the directorate relative to the police and the police minister.[54] Dramat, in turn, decided to take early retirement, for which he received R3 million. This left a vacuum that was filled by Berning Ntlemeza.

Ntlemeza was an extremely controversial choice. A High Court had already found him to be a liar and an unreliable witness, evidence that was simply ignored by Minister Nhleko and the president when they considered him for the position. These facts would later form the basis of a successful challenge to his appointment by the Helen Suzman Foundation and Freedom Under Law, both civil society organisations focused on defending South Africa's Constitution.[55]

What stands out is that Ntlemeza wasted no time in pursuing criminal charges against the minister of finance, Pravin Gordhan (and the individuals implicated in the so-called SARS 'rogue' unit, news of which had broken in October 2014, a month after Tom Moyane had been appointed SARS commissioner).[56] The charge that, as commissioner of SARS, Gordhan had committed fraud by unlawfully approving an early retirement payment to his former deputy, Ivan Pillay, seemed a frivolous matter for a priority crime unit to pursue. As it turns out, the Hawks had either overlooked or withheld vital evidence that exonerated both the minister and Pillay. Ultimately the NPA, despite having made a very public announcement to the contrary, declined to go to trial.[57] The prospect of a trial evaporated and, with it, the excuse to remove Gordhan from the finance portfolio.

Hovering over all these proceedings is the shadow of South Africa's intelligence services. In 2014 Jane Duncan described how 'conveniently leaked intelligence reports, or documents that are claimed to be intelligence reports, have been used to smear those that are considered threats to the current political establishment'.[58] She saw this as part of 'the creeping use of security services to suppress social and political dissent' in what she called a developing 'national security state'.[59] Indeed, the first report of a 'rogue unit' appeared in an article by Jacques Pauw describing an illegal intelligence unit that had sought to discredit the NPA's Glynnis Breytenbach. 'According to a recording in the possession of *City Press*,' Pauw had written,

> members of the Special Operations Unit concocted a story that Breytenbach was a former agent of Israeli intelligence agency Mossad. They then leaked the information to the media to discredit her. The information was repeated by her National Prosecuting Authority bosses when motivating why she should be charged with corruption.[60]

Curiously, Pauw's piece appeared on the same day as the *Sunday Times* ran its own story of a 'rogue unit' – this time at SARS. There is an uncanny similarity between the details, raising the suggestion that the original story had been 'spun' to distract attention from the State Security Agency.

Pauw's story was especially credible given the context. In 2008 then Minister of Intelligence Ronnie Kasrils had commissioned an investigation into the various services. The concern at the time was that 'politicians and intelligence officers can abuse [their] powers to infringe rights without good cause, interfere in lawful politics and favour or prejudice a political party or leader, thereby subverting democracy'.[61]

The report, by former Deputy Security Minister Joe Matthews, former National Assembly speaker Frene Ginwala and Professor Laurie Nathan, director of the Centre for Mediation in Africa in the Department of Political Sciences at the University of Pretoria, found severe shortcomings in the National Strategic Intelligence Act (No. 39 of 1994), which created opportunities for abuse by defining the notion of 'national security' too broadly. Pauw has subsequently gone further in an explosive book that puts new information into the public domain regarding the politicisation of the intelligence services.[62]

The report found that there were no rules regulating counter-intelligence work, making it easy to interfere in politics and infringe rights without sufficient cause.[63] In a finding that surely calls into question the rationale of the Hawks' own 'Crimes Against the State' unit, Matthews, Ginwala and Nathan noted that 'in a democracy it is wholly inappropriate for an intelligence service to make judgements on whether lawful activities are threats to the constitutional order'.[64]

Siyabonga Cwele, who succeeded Ronnie Kasrils as minister of intelligence, sought to suppress this report and the recommendations were not implemented. By 2014 Piet Coetzer, Stef Terblanche and Garth Cilliers, writing for the *Intelligence Bulletin*, were describing the State Security Agency as being in 'disarray'.[65] It is in this context that the various intelligence-like dossiers discussed above started to appear.

The formal link to the State Security Agency is suggested by the story of Mandisa Mokwena, who was recruited into the senior management of SARS from one of its sub-structures, the National Intelligence Agency. Ivan Pillay subsequently charged her with fraud, though the case has never come to court. She subsequently returned to the intelligence fraternity.

Mokwena was probably one of the authors of the infamous 'Spiderweb report' alleging a conspiracy by Gordhan, Pillay and Van Loggerenberg, among others, to marginalise black staff at the agency. In a further twist, Mandisa Mokwena is married to Barnard Mokwena, the former human resources manager at Lonmin, who played a central role in driving a labour dispute at the Marikana mine into the worst massacre of the post-apartheid period. It later emerged that he, too, was an intelligence operative.[66]

The role played by the NPA in enforcing the law (particularly with respect to holding public servants to account for fraud or corruption) cannot be understated.

Since Shaun Abrahams's appointment as National Director of Public Prosecutions in June 2015 several questionable decisions have been made and actions taken, over and above the frivolous charges laid against Gordhan. These include the charges against Robert McBride and the withdrawal of charges of perjury against Nomgcobo Jiba.[67] According to an amaBhungane article, 'Jiba was roundly criticised by judges during her tenure as acting prosecutions head in three separate cases – all of them politically sensitive – leading to accusations that she was protecting President Jacob Zuma or his allies'.[68]

Taken together, the events at SARS, the Hawks and the NPA suggest that as the Zuma administration resorted increasingly to extra-legal means to pursue radical economic transformation, it was driven to 'capture' and weaken key state institutions. The political project of the Zuma-centred power elite has come at a very heavy price for the capability, integrity and stability of the South African state.

Notes and references

1   Turok, B. 2008. *From the Freedom Charter to Polokwane: The Evolution of ANC Economic Policy*: 10. Cape Town: New Agenda.

2   Cosatu. 2002. 'Theory of transition'. Available at: http://amadlandawonye.wikispaces.com/Theory+of+the+Transition%2C+COSATU%2C+Feb+2002.

3   ANCYL. 2010. 'Political report'. Available at: http://www.ancyl.org.za/docs/reps/2010/politicalreportk.html.

4   Cosatu. 2002. 'Theory of transition'.

5   McCrudden, C. 2004. 'Using public procurement to achieve social outcomes'. *Natural Resources Forum: A United Nations Sustainable Development Journal* 28(4): 249–348.

6   See *Review of African Political Economy*, June 1976.

7   Silva, M & G Scott. 2014. 'Empowering small and medium-sized enterprises (SMEs) by leveraging public procurement'. Available at: www.iisd.org/sites/default/files/publications/empowering-smes-eight-big-ideas-mexico.pdf.

8   Taylor, T K & M A Yülek. n.d. 'Leveraging international public procurement in support of economic development: Forecasting public sector expenditures and market size in Turkey': 2436. Available at: www.ippa.org/IPPC5/Proceedings/Part9/PAPER9-6.pdf.

9   Department of Economic Development. 2011. *The New Growth Path*.

10 DTI. 2011. 'Leveraging public procurement. Annual small business summit'. Available at: www.theDTI.gov.za/sme_development/sumit/Leveraging%20Public%20Procurement%20as%20a%20Market%20for%20Small%20Enterprises.pdf.

11   DTI. 2014. 'The DTI to create 100 Black industrialists in three years'. Available at:
     www.theDTI.gov.za/editmedia.jsp?id=3106v.

12   DTI. 2014. 'The DTI to create 100 Black industrialists'.

13   South African Government. 2014. 'Minister Malusi Gigaba: Black Management Forum
     business breakfast' (emphasis added). Available at: www.gov.za/address-minister-malusi-
     gigaba-mp-occasion-business-breakfast-hosted-black-management-forum-bmf .

14   Public Affairs Research Institute. 2014. *The Contract State: Outsourcing and Decentralisation
     in Contemporary South Africa*: 16. Johannesburg: Public Affairs Research Institute. See also
     Brunette, R. Forthcoming. 'Zumaism as machine politics radicalised'; Brunette,
     R, J Klaaren & P Nqaba. Forthcoming. 'The contract state: Towards a fiscal sociology of
     public procurement in South Africa'.

15   Public Affairs Research Institute. 2014. *The Contract State*: 16.

16   Chipkin, I. 2016. *The State, Capture and Revolution in Contemporary South Africa*.
     Johannesburg: Public Affairs Research Institute.

17   Politicsweb. 2014. 'On the ANC's 2014 election manifesto – Jacob Zuma'. Available at:
     www.politicsweb.co.za/news-and-analysis/on-the-ancs-2014-election-manifesto – jacob-
     zuma.

18   Technical Assistance Unit. 2012. 'Diagnostic research report on corruption,
     non-compliance and weak organisations'. Prepared by the Public Affairs Research Institute.
     Available at: www.pari.org.za/wp-content/uploads/Diagnostic-corruption-TAU-PARI-
     FINAL-24Oct2012-2.pdf.

19   Office of the Chief Procurement Officer. n.d. 'About us'. Available at: ocpo.treasury.gov.za/
     About_Us/Pages/The-Chief-Procurement-Officer.aspx.

20   Lodge, T. 2014. 'Neo-patrimonial politics in the ANC'. *African Affairs* 113(463): 1.

21   Lodge. 2014. 'Neo-patrimonial politics': 57.

22   Lodge. 2014. 'Neo-patrimonial politics': 57.

23   Lodge. 2014. 'Neo-patrimonial politics': 57.

24   Republic of South Africa. 1996. *The Constitution of the Republic of South
     Africa*: Section 217 (1), (2). Pretoria: Republic of South Africa.

25   The Sunday Independent. 2016. 'Treasury rules continue to betray black entrepreneurs'.
     Available at: www.pressreader.com/south-africa/the-sunday-independent/
     20160703/282054801349421.

26   DTI. 2013. 'The National Broad-Based Black Economic Empowerment Summit. A decade of
     economic empowerment – (2003–2013). Summit report': 30. Available at: www.DTI.gov.za/
     economic_empowerment/docs/National_Summit_Report.pdf.

27   Malikane, C. 2017. 'Concerning the current situation'. Available at: http://blackopinion.
     co.za/2017/04/26/concerning-current-situation-proposal-professor-chris-malikane/.

28   Malikane. 2017. 'Current situation'.

29   Malikane. 2017. 'Current situation'.

30 See, for example, the ANC's 2017 organisational renewal document which argues that during the Mbeki period there was 'marked progress towards a National Democratic Society'. The reason for this was that economic growth was relatively quick, fiscal expenditure on social and other services grew dramatically and civil society activism was strong. Most noteworthy is the ANC's suggestion that 'institutions tasked with defending and promoting the Constitution sought to play their role, with the judiciary standing out among them in asserting its independence and a progressive interpretation of the provisions of the Constitution'. This was a far cry from the suggestion that the Constitution was an obstacle to progressive transformation in South Africa. (ANC. 2017. 'Organisation renewal and organisational design discussion document'. 5th National Policy Conference 30 June–5 July 2017, Gallagher Convention Centre, Midrand, Gauteng, South Africa.)

31 National Treasury. 2017. *Budget Review*: 92. Available at: www.treasury. gov.za/documents/national%20budget/2017/review/FullBR.pdf.

32 Given the secrecy surrounding the nuclear deal, this was hardly surprising. The High Court has ruled that all current initiatives to procure nuclear power are unconstitutional and, therefore, null and void. The court's major objection seems to have been the way negotiations bypassed Parliament and the lack of public consultation and scrutiny of their terms.

33 See Wright, J, T Bischof-Niemz, J Calitz & M Crescent. 2016. 'Least-cost electricity mix for South Africa until 2040'. CSIR Energy Centre, Johannesburg. Presentation at a Nelson Mandela Foundation dialogue, 14 November.

34 National Treasury. 2009. 'Supply chain management: Request for public comments. Draft preferential procurement regulations, 2009 aligned with the aims of the Broad-Based Black Economic Empowerment Act and its related strategy'. Available at: www.treasury.gov.za/divisions/ocpo/sc/PPPFA/letter%20dep%20bbbeeooo1.pdf.

35 Government Gazette. 2011. 'R. 501 Preferential Procurement Policy Framework Act (5/2000): Notice in terms of Section 1 (iii) (f)'. Available at: www.treasury.gov.za/divisions/ocpo/sc/PPPFA/1-34350%208-6%20NatTreas.pdf.

36 Government Gazette. 2011. 'R. 1027 Preferential Procurement Policy Framework Act (5/2000): Exemptions from the application of the Preferential Procurement Regulations, 2011': 3. Available at: www.treasury.gov.za/divisions/ocpo/sc/PPPFA/1-34832%207-12%20NatTreas.pdf.

37 Hogan had gone on record saying that as minister of public enterprises she had come under political pressure to broker a Gupta-related deal with SAA.

38 Public Protector South Africa. 2016. *State of Capture*.

39 Public Protector South Africa. 2016. *State of Capture*.

40 Public Protector South Africa. 2016. *State of Capture*.

41 Public Affairs Research Institute. 2016. 'State capture at a local level'. Available at: http://pari.org.za/wp-content/uploads/Crispian-Olver_State-Capture-at-a-Local-Level-Case-of-NMB_Working-Paper_Nov-16.pdf.

42   Chipkin, I. 2015. 'The state capture and revolution in contemporary South Africa'. Available at: http://pari.org.za/wp-content/uploads/The-State-Capture-and-Revolution-in-Contemporary-South-Africa-1.pdf.

43   ANC. 2017. 'Organisation renewal discussion document'.

44   ANC. 2017. 'Organisation renewal discussion document': 90, 134, 135, 136.

45   Naidoo, V. 2017. 'Tracking South Africa's expansionary state, 1994–2010: Re-tooling the machinery of government'. Cape Town: Department of Political Science, University of Cape Town.

46   Naidoo. 2017. 'Tracking South Africa's expansionary state': 24.

47   Chipkin. 2016. *The State, Capture and Revolution*: 13.

48   Phadi, M & J Pearson. 2017. *The Mogalakwena Local Municipality in South Africa: An Institutional Case-Study*. Johannesburg: Public Affairs Research Institute.

49   For a brief overview of the history of SARS, see Hausman, D. 2010. *Reworking the Revenue Service: Tax Collection in South Africa, 1999–2009*. Princeton University: Innovations for Successful Societies.

50   Van Loggerenberg, J & A Lackay. 2016. *Rogue: The Inside Story of SARS's Elite Crime-Busting Unit*. Johannesburg & Cape Town: Jonathan Ball Publishers.

51   Timeslive.co.za. 2016. 'SARS and the *Sunday Times*: Our response'. Available at: www.timeslive.co.za/sundaytimes/opinion/2016/04/03/SARS-and-the-Sunday-Times-our-response1.

52   Thamm, M. 2015. 'Press Ombudsman's rulings against *Sunday Times* vindicate Pillay and van Loggerenberg'. Available at: www.dailymaverick.co.za/article/2015-12-16-press-ombudsmans-rulings-against-sunday-times-vindicate-sars-officials/.

53   Thamm, M. 2017. 'Zuma committed perjury, former NPA head Nxasana claims in affidavit'. Available at: www.dailymaverick.co.za/article/2017-04-13-zuma-committed-perjury-former-npa-head-nxasana-claims-in-affidavit/#.WQofKhN9600.

54   South Africa Constitutional Court. 2016. *McBride v Minister of Police and Another (CCT255/15)*. Available at: www.saflii.org/za/cases/ZACC/2016/30.html.

55   Mail & Guardian. 2017. 'Court sets aside appointment of Berning Ntlemeza'. Available at: mg.co.za/article/2017-03-17-breaking-court-sets-aside-appointment-of-berning-ntlemeza.

56   Despite the lengthy investigation it seems that there is still insufficient evidence to support charges relating to the 'rogue unit' allegations.

57   Since 2010 the leadership of the NPA has been the site of major contestation, as have the cases it has chosen or declined to prosecute. Much of this was related to the criminal charges brought against Zuma arising from the notorious arms deal. Some cases, however, may have related to procurement violations and/or illegality linked to activities connected to radical economic transformation.

58   Duncan, J. 2014. *The Rise of the Securocrats: The Case of South Africa*: 3. Johannesburg: Jacana Media.

59   Duncan. 2014. *The Rise of the Securocrats*: 32.

60 Pauw, J. 2014. 'How spy unit nailed Mdluli foes'. Available at: www.pressreader.com/ south-africa/citypress/20140810/281638188364837.

61 Ministerial Review Commission on Intelligence. 2008. 'Intelligence in a constitutional democracy': 10.

62 Pauw, J. 2017. *The President's Keepers: Those Keeping Zuma in Power and out of Prison.* Cape Town: Tafelberg.

63 Ministerial Review Commission on Intelligence. 2008. 'Intelligence in a constitutional democracy'.

64 Ministerial Review Commission on Intelligence. 2008. 'Intelligence in a constitutional democracy': 134.

65 Coetzer, P, S Terblanche & G Cilliers. 2014. 'Political abuse has State Security Agency in disarray'. Available at: www.theintelligencebulletin.co.za/articles/security-watch-1812.html.

66 Marinovich, G. 2016. *Murder at Small Koppie: The Real Story of the Marikana Massacre.* Cape Town: Penguin Books.

67 Van Wyk, P. 2016. 'NPA's Nomgcobo Jiba and Lawrence Mrwebi struck off the roll of advocates'. Available at: https://mg.co.za/article/2016-09-15-npas-nomgcobo-jiba-and-lawrence-mrwebi-struck-from-the-roll-for-advocates.

68 Sole, S. 2016. 'Willie's shock gambit ups the stakes at NPA'. Available at: amabhungane.co.za/article/2016-02-05-willies-shock-gambit-ups-the-stakes-at-npa.

5

Conclusion

State capture by shadowy elites has profound implications for state institutions. It destroys public trust in the state and its organs, it weakens key economic agencies that are tasked with delivering development outcomes, and it erodes confidence in the economy.

When there is no trust in public institutions there is little incentive to pay tax; large companies sit on cash rather than reinvest profits towards productive use; criminality proliferates, exploiting weaknesses in intelligence and crime enforcement authorities; and both capital and skills flee the country. The majority of South Africans are bearing the brunt of these corrosive developments.

In the previous chapters we have documented the systematic repurposing of state institutions by the Zuma-centred power elite. These premeditated and coordinated activities are designed to enrich a core group of beneficiaries, to consolidate political power and to ensure the long-term survival of the rent-seeking system that has been built by this power elite over the past decade. To this end a symbiotic relationship between the constitutional state and the shadow state has been built and consolidated.

At the nexus of this symbiosis is a handful of companies and individuals connected in one way or another to the Gupta–Zuma family network. Decisions made within this nexus are executed by well-placed individuals located in the most significant centres of state power (in government, SOEs and the bureaucracy).

Former Deputy Minister of Finance Mcebisi Jonas told the public protector that he had been offered a place in this network with a R600 million bribe. This transaction reveals the clear modus operandi of those who operate within the shadow state, and how this has made it possible for them to gain control of the constitutional state.

Crucially, we have no idea how many others accepted these kinds of unimaginably enormous bribes. Those who resist are systematically removed, redeployed to other lucrative positions to silence them, placed under tremendous pressure, or hounded out by trumped up internal and/or external charges and dubious intelligence reports.

We have argued that the attempts by the Zuma-centred power elite to centralise the control of rents in order to eliminate lower-order rent-seeking competitors began in about 2012. The ultimate prize was control of the National Treasury, because this would give them control of the Financial Intelligence Centre, the Chief Procurement Office (which regulates procurement and activates legal action against corrupt practices), and the Public Investment Corporation (the second-largest shareholder on the Johannesburg Stock Exchange), and the power to issue guarantees (which is essential for making the nuclear deal work). The Cabinet reshuffle in April 2017 was the final step taken to make possible control of the National Treasury.

The capture of the National Treasury, however, followed four other processes that consolidated power and centralised control of rents: the ballooning of the Senior Management Service in the public service to create a compliant, politically dependent bureaucratic class; the routing of the good cops from the police and intelligence services and their replacement with loyalists prepared to cover up illegal rent seeking; redirection of the procurement spend of the SOEs to favour those who were prepared to deal with the Gupta–Zuma network of brokers; and the consolidation of the 'Premier League' as a network of party bosses to ensure that the NEC of the ANC remains loyal, because it is implicated in the flow of large amounts of cash to keep this political Ponzi scheme going.

At the epicentre of the political project is a rhetorical commitment to radical economic transformation. Unsurprisingly, although the ANC's official policy documents on radical economic transformation encompass a broad range of interventions that take the NDP as a point of departure, the Zuma-centred power elite has emphasised the role of the SOEs and, in particular, the procurement spend of the SOEs. Eskom and Transnet are the centrepieces of this focus: Eskom because it is regarded as key to ensuring that the nuclear deal goes ahead, and Transnet because it is regarded as key to ensuring that the mining industry is captured and Transnet properties are released to a select group of private companies.

In short, instead of becoming a new economic policy consensus, radical economic transformation has been turned into an ideological football kicked around by factional political players within the ANC itself and the Tripartite Alliance in general, who use the term to mean very different things. Crucially, radical economic transformation is used to give ideological legitimacy to what is essentially a political project to repurpose state institutions for the benefit of a power elite.

Three things need to happen if the crisis is to be resolved.

Firstly, the Gupta–Zuma network must be broken and dismantled. This will require political action within and outside the Tripartite Alliance. Zuma has been dislodged as the kingpin. However, this must be coupled with legal action to criminalise and bring the perpetrators of state capture to justice. To a large extent, this had happened by the end of 2017, resulting in major political shifts.

To this end, the public protector's recommendation that a judicial commission of inquiry be established has now been implemented. The commission will be chaired by the deputy chief justice. This is a major step forward. It will also require bold action by the banking sector and the Reserve Bank to expose and shut down the financial mechanisms that the shadow state uses. The closing of the Oakbay company accounts was a brave step, but it does not go far enough.

Secondly, a new national economic consensus is required. This has never been given serious attention beyond setting out multiple policy frameworks and bureaucratic processes. The short-lived post-1994 RDP developed by the Presidency was unilaterally replaced in 1996 by the Gear policy – a framework developed by the Ministry of Finance and adopted without the approval of the Alliance partners. At the same time the Department of Labour's Presidential Labour Market Commission came up with a social plan. A few years later ASGISA was also adopted without full consensus. The adoption in 2002 of the 'developmental state' framework came closest to a consensus, but it lacked substance and focused primarily on a weakly defined industrial policy framework, one that has failed to induce confidence in the economy and public investment in infrastructure as a way of 'crowding in' private investment.

The subsequent adoption of the New Growth Path did not improve matters, especially when this was interpreted by Gigaba, after he was appointed minister of public enterprises in 2010, as a licence to transform the governance of the SOEs. The economic policies inscribed in ASGISA also never enjoyed the full support of the Alliance partners, not least because the NDP is pessimistic about the future of manufacturing, saying virtually nothing about de-financialisation, and is vague when it comes to achieving employment-centred development in an environment where trade unions have policy influence.

While the external environment in the wake of the global financial crisis has certainly had adverse effects on South Africa's growth outlook, governance failures and policy uncertainty have inflicted the most damage. Promises made by the ANC to its Alliance partners after the final draft of the NDP was published that there would be further efforts to strengthen the economic policies of the NDP were never carried out. The DTI industrial policy framework adopted in 2007 was resisted by National Treasury, which argued against 'picking winners', thus thwarting the implementation of industrial policy.

In short, there has never really been a broadly shared and fully supported economic policy framework. Radical economic transformation is already a factional political football. One can speculate that a positive outcome of this political crisis would be the adoption, for the first time ever, of a new economic consensus that can unite the different factions of the Alliance by giving real substance to radical economic transformation while enjoying broad stakeholder support in the business community, labour sector and civil society. Without this, the power elite that formed around Zuma will be able to continue co-opting radical economic transformation in order to mask ongoing rent-seeking practices by manipulating SOE procurement spend. This is unlikely to crowd in private investment.

The nuclear deal will probably be justified in terms of radical economic transformation, masking how Eskom's procurement system and the issuing of a sovereign guarantee will be used to effectively hand over the South African economy to (Russian) foreign interests. The nuclear deal is the ultimate 'big and shiny' capital-intensive project that reinforces the minerals-energy complex, crowds out investment in the cheapest energy available (which is renewable energy), increases indebtedness to foreign lenders and, of course, benefits the cohort of rent-seeking corrupt insiders.

A new economic consensus will have to address the core challenge of investment. As argued in Chapter 2, after 1994 the combination of the shareholder value movement, BEE and financialisation redirected surpluses away from productive employment-creating investments. Since they were adopted in 2007, industrial policies have not had much success beyond defending the position of the automotive sector and limited successes in the clothing and textile sector. These two sectors remain vulnerable in the face of global competitive challenges from other developing countries as well as risks relating to the longevity of the African Growth and Opportunity Act, which has been a boon for the auto sector. The introduction of the 100 Black Industrialists programme has diverted focus from implementing good industrial policy strategies. It would seem that the Black Industrialists scheme, as good as it looks on paper, has been poorly administered, with very little value created thus far.

Compared to its peers in the rest of the world, South Africa has, since 1994, been an anomaly. High returns on investment are usually associated with high investment levels, as is the case with China. In South Africa returns on investment have been similar to those of China, but investment levels – and therefore employment-creation rates – are low. This is partly the result of market concentration that gives large conglomerates more market power to extract higher margins than would have been possible in a more competitive environment, and partly caused by the fact that the business class, which remains dominated by white decision-makers, has a low level of confidence in the post-1994 democratic project. Even international financial institutions such as the International Monetary Fund have underlined the concentration of product markets as problematic and in need of deep reforms. The use of SOE procurement spend has tended to strengthen investment in large capital-intensive projects concentrated within the minerals-energy complex. This reinforces a pattern of job-starved economic growth in an economy with one of the highest unemployment rates in the world. What is really needed, therefore, is employment- and livelihood-creating investments across a wide spectrum of small and medium enterprises capable of absorbing large numbers of unskilled and semi-skilled workers. This, however, will need to be supported by a proliferation of innovations that emerge from what are often referred to as 'triple helix' innovation networks (partnerships among enterprises, knowledge institutions and state institutions) that connect knowledge and market opportunities with investment flows and an enabling regulatory environment.

Innovative policy, which 'creatively destroys' to engender new forms of economic development, lies at the heart of truly inclusive economic growth. This kind of strategy can, however, only be realised if the financialisation of the economy is complemented by, for example, channelling more public funds through South Africa's well-developed development finance institutions, and redirecting the investments of these institutions away from blue-chip companies and capital-intensive projects into higher-risk employment- and livelihood-creating enterprises located in both the private and non-profit sectors.

The third thing that is needed to enable resolution of the crisis is for all stake-holders, in particular the political actors who replace the Zuma-centred power elite in the future, to commit to realising the vision of a new economic consensus within the framework of the Constitution and relevant legislation. The recent trend towards regarding the Constitution and the rule of law (such as the Public Finance

Management Act) as an obstacle to radical economic transformation is dangerous, and must be stopped. Transformation is perfectly compatible with the Constitution and with respect for the judiciary. Indeed, without this, the trust required for 'triple helix'-type employment- and livelihood-centred economic development will not materialise. A new trust compact is required if stakeholders are to work together in meaningful ways.

Afterword

Ferial Haffajee

When the *Betrayal of the Promise* report first came out in May 2017, it was brilliant but bone-chilling. The report set out how South Africa was being run by a shadow state based on the repurposing of state institutions.

Presented in graphics, and with a wonderful mix of academic analysis plaited with the factual findings of investigative journalists, *Betrayal of the Promise* provided meaning in a time of madness. But it was bone-chilling because the process of capture seemed, at the time, to be ineluctable and irreversible, its power captured in each riveting one of the 63 pages. The tentacles of capture were too deep, the godfathers of South Africa too powerful, the then president too engaged in corruption to turn it around. *Betrayal of the Promise* provided a big-picture view of how institutions had been repurposed to suit the crony networks that had come to control and dominate the hundreds of billions of rands available in the procurement budgets of the state and its state-owned companies.

* * *

As an editor and a journalist, and then a researcher at the PARI, it felt as if all that I wrote with my fellow journalists to oppose state capture and corruption amounted to putting a finger in the dyke.

There is an image of the Gupta brothers, taken years ago, which flashes up on the screen to accompany almost every story about them because it was taken at one of the first and only interviews they granted the media. It features Atul and Ajay Gupta with Duduzane Zuma, former President Jacob Zuma's son and the Gupta family's business partner, along with one of their local partners at the time, Jagdish Parekh.

The family had made their first audacious act of capture: one of their earlier companies, Imperial Crown Trading, was competing with Kumba Iron Ore for Arcelor-Mittal's stake in a Sishen mine, and had hijacked mineral rights from Kumba in an act that was comedic but successful. Acolytes of the family had photocopied Kumba's application for rights to mine Sishen, submitted these as their own and won the rights.

At the apogée of their power (President Zuma, their patron, had just been made head of state after a landslide victory at the governing ANC's Polokwane conference in 2007) the brothers were keen on good publicity, and I knew Parekh from university, so they spoke to journalists Adriaan Basson, Muntu Vilakazi and me. What strikes me now about that interview was their lies and bombast, but mostly how their smiles and arrogance reflected the certainty of their power.

The granting of mining rights at Sishen was ultimately overturned in the courts because Kumba put up a battle, and it's interesting that that first foray hardly features in *Betrayal of the Promise*; thereafter the Gupta network executed a plan sketched with Machiavellian insight by Ajay Gupta, the oldest brother and the *capo di tutti capi* of the family. From the attempted theft of mineral rights at Sishen, the family went on to establish an empire which included mining, media, defence, information technology, professional services, asset raising and rail procurement, among many other smaller forays into any sector where relationships and contacts in the state could be leveraged.

It was breathtaking to read and report every single week on what the network was up to – like watching capture economics on steroids. Reporting then felt like an act of resistance, with the amaBhungane Centre for Investigative Journalism leading the guerrilla army of journalists who spent years uncovering the tentacles of the networks. This seemed at the time like a tenuous effort, one with no guarantee of success.

The speed at which the reports were produced was so relentless that the ability to provide a narrative or overarching meaning for them was simply impossible, because the requirements of reporting within the law consumed all our time. Reporting the shadow state was extraordinarily hard work. You had to steer clear of defamation suits; whistleblowers were thin on the ground; it was a time before the #GuptaLeaks emails allowed journalists from amaBhungane, the *Daily Maverick's* Scorpio team and News24 to piece it all together for us as they did in 2017. What *Betrayal of the Promise* did was to build on this investigative work, pulling it all together and providing a set of concepts that made it possible to understand what had happened, and was still happening. The shadow state, the idea of repurposing state institutions, the graphic showing networks that had been created, and the location of the concept of rent seeking within a political ideology were enormously helpful ways to inform the citizenry of the need to think beyond the narrow framework of outrage at corruption. This outrage was not a helpful narrative for a nation tired of all the nonsense – the institutional battles, misuses of funds and legal challenges being reported on an almost daily basis – but without the vocabulary to stage a proper challenge to what was happening. *Betrayal of the Promise* provided the vocabulary and, it turns out, the ammunition.

* * *

I was privileged to read early versions of *Betrayal of the Promise* as we planned the media blitz ahead of its release. I was riveted and energised by it. It was personally helpful because of the direct attacks I had been facing as a result of my reporting work.

Some months before, I had started finding and saving appalling images of myself on Twitter. There was a nascent movement against what was called 'white monopoly capital' on social media, and it targeted journalists who were writing about corruption and its heightened form as practised by the Gupta–Zuma network. A twisted mind had taken images of me and superimposed these on billionaire Johann Rupert's bed, on his lap, and on his cow and dog. The meaning was clear – as a journalist, I was being run by Rupert or white capital to write and report on state capture.

Soon, any journalist who wrote about the crony network's escapades was similarly trolled and abused online. The goading and attacks were unending and relentless, and as the massive misinformation campaign unfolded the stakes became clear. As we now know, the Gupta family had hired the global PR company Bell Pottinger to plan and execute a project to scrub their reputations, and also to run a 'dark ops' campaign to attack their critics using social media.

Betrayal of the Promise allowed me, for the first time, to understand why the Gupta family and their various hired hands had weaponised social media. The stakes were very high, and the relentless investigations had led to growing public opprobrium. *Betrayal of the Promise* allowed for that opprobrium to be turned into a political weapon as the report ricocheted across the country, providing an antidote to the misinformation campaign. This campaign quickly lost ground, as the intellectual rigour and the exhaustive analysis of the report by some of the finest academics in the country came together to pierce the smokescreen of the anti-white monopoly capital and pro-radical economic transformation narrative the Guptas' sophists had cooked up for them. President Jacob Zuma, and Cabinet members who were part of his project of capture and repurposing, had adopted this narrative.

Because *Betrayal of the Promise* was written without rancour and from a progressive perspective, it has been used again and again and again by people within the ANC who were set for the battle royal against the corruption of the Zuma administration. The report was the ammunition used at early parliamentary inquiries into state capture and in several of the biggest court cases used by civil society to batter the network. Its language and framing became part of the lexicon of opposition to corruption and state capture. It became the core document in this process, produced pitch perfect by an unprecedented alliance of public intellectuals in record time to give it power and impact. In *Betrayal of the Promise* lies a precedent, one which can be leveraged again and again as South Africans strive to make the country of our dreams.

* * *

As I read the report again while preparing to write this afterword, it felt as though I was reading it in a different country. South Africa now is an unprecedented arena of accountability for state capture. There are three parliamentary inquiries under way into aspects of corruption at different SOEs. The deputy chief justice of South Africa, Raymond Zondo, has announced his team of commissioners for the judicial commission of inquiry into state capture. Former Public Protector Thuli Madonsela's recommendation for this inquiry is now a living institution. Corruption charges against former President Jacob Zuma relating to his role in the arms deal have been reinstated. He is now *former* president; the era of hopelessness is over, as President Cyril Ramaphosa faces a nation insisting that he make good on his stump promise to be an anti-corruption leader.

The Asset Forfeiture Unit at the NPA has opened what it says are hundreds of cases into state capture, and the Gupta brothers, Ajay and Atul, are now fugitives from justice. Wanted by the Hawks for their role in theft from a Free State dairy project called Estina, the brothers are, at the time of writing, on the run in their private jet *ZSOAK*. They have removed the tracking device from the jet because South Africa's army of Twitter detectives was using smart aviators to report on where and when the plane moved, so that the family could be tracked whether they were in Dubai or India. In both those countries, law enforcement agencies have pledged to act against the Guptas. This is less likely to happen in Dubai, which is a known haven for illicit money, but in India tax authorities have already swooped on the family's homes and businesses. They are not in jail, but they have lost face and name, both of which have been large elements of their identity and their sense of self.

* * *

It would be naïve to think that it is game, set and match to the forces opposed to state capture. In its conclusion, *Betrayal of the Promise* recorded that at the nexus of this symbiosis between the constitutional and shadow states are multiple companies – some set up as shells, others as operational entities, some operating domestically, others multi-jurisdictionally – and tens of individuals, meticulously positioned in the classic 'war economy' model as patrons, elites, brokers or dealers – all connected in one way or another to the Gupta–Zuma family network. The way this is strategically coordinated constitutes the shadow state. While the various inquiries into state capture feel omnipresent, as do the regular news reports about the actions of the Asset Forfeiture Unit and the Hawks, these have not yet touched sides to disable the network.

Betrayal of the Promise goes on to record that 'the official testimony to the Public Protector by former Deputy Minister of Finance Mcebisi Jonas – that has not been successfully or credibly contested – is about how he was offered a place in this network with a R600-million bribe. This transaction reveals the clear modus operandi of those who operate within the shadow state and how this has made it possible for them to gain control of the constitutional state.' And here's the important part for our consideration in the aftermath of the era of capture: 'Crucially, we, in turn, have no idea how many others accepted these kinds of unimaginably enormous bribes. Those who resist this agenda are systematically removed, redeployed to other lucrative positions to silence them, placed under tremendous pressure, or hounded out by trumped-up internal and/or external charges and dubious intelligence reports.'[1] There is a lot about the shadow state that is not known – including which politicians and public servants took the huge bribes we now know were proffered.

Moreover, a weekly deep dive into local and regional media will show that the Gupta–Zuma network may have been the most pernicious and powerful, but it is not the only one. There are concentric networks operating across South Africa and across all three spheres of the state – local, provincial and national. Wherever there is a public procurement system, there are networks arranged to take advantage of them. Crispian Olver's book *How to Steal a City*, based on the time he spent as an ANC deployee to Nelson Mandela Bay Municipality, offers deep insight into how local networks are deployed and how systems of government have been repurposed to serve the ends of organised political crime.[2] There are political mafias everywhere, and President Cyril Ramaphosa will have to work with extreme assiduousness to begin to unwind these.

His task will be made more difficult by the fact that he came to party power at the ANC conference at Nasrec in Johannesburg in December 2017 by the slimmest of margins – just 179 votes stood between him and his opponent, Nkosazana Dlamini-Zuma. He was helped to victory when the Mpumalanga premier, David Mabuza, threw his political weight and support base behind the #CR17 campaign. Mabuza is reforming himself before taking a tilt at the ANC presidency in 2027, but it's worth remembering that he has perfected the system of provincial capture in ways that make the Gupta network look positively amateur. He is now the deputy president of South Africa.

Betrayal of the Promise formed part of what is a nascent countervailing force in South Africa. This powerful anti-corruption movement saw journalists, civil society organisations and academics come together with organic mass movements to stage a multi-front battle against state capture. In the end, the sheer force, resources and energy thrown into this battle led to its success. There's no doubt in my mind that this force, shaped outside the ANC, helped to secure a victory for Ramaphosa and for his anti-corruption ticket.

This tells me a story. The solution to excavating the extent of state capture and to keeping up the vigilance will lie with this new force, rather than being entrusted to politics alone.

Notes and references

1 Bhorat et al. 2017. *Betrayal of the Promise*: 61.
2 Olver, C. 2017. *How to Steal a City*. Johannesburg: Jonathan Ball.

Contributors

Haroon Bhorat is professor of economics and director of the Development Policy Research Unit at the University of Cape Town. His research interests cover labour economics, poverty and income distribution. He has served as an economic advisor to past ministers of finance and holds a National Research Chair. He is a Non-resident Senior Fellow at the Brookings Institution, sits on the World Bank's Advisory Board of the Commission on Global Poverty, and was head of research for the United Nations High-Level Panel on the Post-2015 Development Agenda.

Mbongiseni Buthelezi is research manager at the Public Affairs Research Institute. He works on issues of governance, traditional authorities and the state in South Africa. He holds a PhD in English and Comparative Literature from Columbia University and previously held various teaching and research positions at the University of Cape Town.

Ivor Chipkin is the founding director of the Public Affairs Research Institute linked to the University of the Witwatersrand and the University of Cape Town, which has been a pioneer in the field of institutional studies in South Africa, bringing social science methods to the study of government and how it works. He is also an associate professor at the University of the Witwatersrand. He spent four years in the Democracy and Governance Programme at the Human Sciences Research Council, where he acquired an intimate knowledge of government departments and agencies. In 2007 he published *Do South Africans Exist? Nationalism, Democracy and the Identity of 'the People'* (Wits University Press), and has also published widely on questions of government, governance and the state in South Africa.

Sikhulekile Duma is a master's student in Sustainable Development at the University of Stellenbosch. He is also a researcher at the University of Stellenbosch's Centre for Complex Systems in Transitions. His research focus areas include state transformation, state-led investments and the political economy of the South African energy sector. He has an interest in politics, civic engagement and South African political economy.

Hannah Friedenstein (pseudonym) is a financial crime risk specialist and a former journalist. She advises investors entering the African market from a reputation and financial crime risk perspective, as well as working in the civic space against state capture and corruption.

Lumkile Mondi is a senior lecturer in the School of Economics and Business Science at the University of the Witwatersrand. His research interests include political economy, public finance and macroeconomics. He is a respected thought leader in South Africa and throughout the region, where he writes and presents commentaries on African political economy in the print media and on radio and television.

Camaren Peter is an independent researcher and writer based in Cape Town. He is a physicist by training, but has collaborated across a wide range of disciplinary boundaries over the past two decades. His research is mainly focused on leadership, policy and planning for sustainable development in developing-world contexts. His writing deals with themes ranging from memory to forgiveness, reconciliation, ethics, freedom, disruption and the need for a transition to a new politics and society.

Nicky Prins is a former chief director of the Capital Projects Appraisal Unit at the National Treasury in South Africa, where she spent nine years. Previously, she worked as an editor and economist for the Economist Intelligence Unit and for Dunn and Bradstreet Country Risk Services in the UK. She now works as a freelance analyst, focusing on understanding 'business unusual' practices in South Africa's state-owned entities, in support of efforts to combat corruption.

Mzukisi Qobo is an expert and thought leader on governance, leadership and global political economy. He is associate professor and deputy director at the NRF Research Chair on African Diplomacy and Foreign Policy, University of Johannesburg. He has in the past fulfilled leadership roles that span government, policy think tanks and academia, and is currently a project leader on a programme aimed at helping the South African government to undertake risk assessment related to money laundering and corrupt practices, and to fulfil its commitments to the G20 High Level Principles on Transparency in Beneficial Ownership. In his former role as chief director responsible for trade policy at the Department of Trade and Industry, he drafted South Africa's current trade policy. He is also a columnist for the *Daily Maverick*, and serves on the Board of Corruption Watch.

Mark Swilling is Distinguished Professor in Sustainable Development at the University of Stellenbosch. He is the coordinator of the Masters and Doctoral Programme: Sustainable Development in the School of Public Leadership, co-director of the Centre for Complex Systems in Transition, and co-founder and academic director of the Sustainability Institute. The primary research focus of his career can be defined as 'societal transitions' within the wider discipline of sustainability science and governance, with a particular contextual focus on urban sustainability. His published research has been coupled to major institution-building collaborations – an achievement that was recognised in 2010 when he was awarded the Aspen Faculty Pioneer Award for success in introducing sustainability into leadership education. He has published several books including (with Eve Annecke) *Just Transitions: Explorations of Sustainability in an Unfair World* (United Nations University Press, 2012); *Untamed Urbanisms* (co-edited with Adriana Allen and Andrea Lampis, Routledge, 2015); and *Greening the South African Economy* (co-edited with Josephine Musango and Jeremy Wakeford, Juta, 2016).

Index

CPSIA information can be obtained
at www.ICGtesting.com
Printed in the USA
BVHW03s1321280918
528781BV00001B/23/P